ST ALBION
PARISH NEWS

BOOK 4

PREFACE BY THE VICAR

Well, goodness me, this is the fourth collection of my Parish Newsletters to be published in as many years! At this rate there will be a *dozen* on the shelf before I am through!

Only joking, of course, I am not so vain as to keep them all on a shelf!

But they do seem to be popular and if my humble offerings help in some major way to make the world a better place, then who am I to stop people enjoying them!

So here it is, the fourth gospel according to Tony!

Only joking, of course, I am not so vain as to think that my newsletters are like the old-fashioned gospels – those books were riddled with inconsistencies and inaccuracies for a start!

Yours as ever (and for ever!)

Tony

Published in Great Britain by
Private Eye Productions Ltd, 6 Carlisle Street, W1D 3BN.
© 2001 Pressdram Ltd
ISBN 1 901784 25 8
Designed by Bridget Tisdall
Printed in England by Ebenezer Baylis & Son Ltd, Worcester
2 4 6 8 10 9 7 5 3 1

MORE VICAR ANYONE?

ST ALBION PARISH NEWS
BOOK 4

Further letters from the vicar,
the Rev. A.R.P. Blair MA (Oxon)

compiled for

PRIVATE EYE

by Ian Hislop, Richard Ingrams,
Christopher Booker and Barry Fantoni

ST ALBION PARISH NEWS

22nd September 2000

Hullo!

And a pretty angry "hullo" it is too!

This newsletter will be reaching you all rather late, since Mrs Roche, who delivers them, ran out of petrol on Wednesday.

And whose fault was that, may I ask? A tiny minority of selfish, irresponsible, and thoroughly selfish individuals whose only concern has been to get something for nothing!

They were prepared to stop at nothing to get it, however much they inconvenienced everybody else. They were quite happy to put at risk the lives of the frail, the elderly and toddlers.

I was shocked when I went into Tesco in the High Street and saw that the shelves were empty.

As a familiar voice put it to me from the check-out queue, "Give us this day our daily bread, Vicar. Isn't that your job? Well, where is it then?"

I thought this was pretty rich coming from someone who had filled his trolley to bursting with every conceivable type of loaf, including Cornish Soda Bread, the Wensleydale Cob and the Organic Ciabatta.

"O ye of little fuel" *(BP Book of Shell 7.3)*

"Man cannot live by bread alone," I told him, quoting from the Book of Crises. "Quite right, Vicar," he said. "I must get the last of those baked beans as well."

Isn't this just typical of the mindless selfishness which seems to have swept through the whole parish in recent days, like some biblical plague of yore.

Many of you even seem to have expected me to give my blessing to this tiny minority of troublemakers just because the whole parish was silly enough to support them.

Well, let me tell you, in the words of Our Lady of Handbags, the Blessed Margaret, "The Vicar is not for turning"!

Listen, here is a parable which everyone in the parish should take to heart. It is the story of the Wise and Foolish Virgins, who in the Bible were confronted with a fuel crisis because the international price of oil had gone up by three times.

One lot of virgins, the wise ones, just stayed at home and did not exacerbate the situation.

But the foolish ones immediately rushed out and indulged in panic-buying to keep their lamps full of oil.

As a direct result of this action, toddlers' lives were put at risk. How selfish can you get?

So I hope that's given you all something to think about! It is lucky that on this occasion there was a happy ending, because someone, ie your Vicar, was prepared to show a bit of moral leadership!

As soon as I made it clear that I was not prepared to tolerate this kind of conduct in the parish for even one more day, the whole thing fizzled out in just over a week. So much for the so-called crisis!

Yours more in anger than in sorrow,

Tony

PS. If any parishioner happens to have a spare can of Super Unleaded, may I remind them that "spreading the Good News" is an "emergency service"!

Harvest Festival

Our Harvest Festival service this year has been cancelled, as there is nothing left in the shops to bring in. T.B.

FROM THE WORKING MEN'S CLUB – AN ANNOUNCEMENT

I deeply regret to have to tell our members that as from midnight last night there was not a single drop of beer left in the club. I blame that bloody twit of a vic

We regret that Mr Prescott's announcement has been cut due to the fuel crisis. A.C.

Valete

It's farewell to **Mrs Mowlam**, known to some of you as "St Mo"! We're all very sad to lose someone who has contributed so much to the life of the parish in so many ways, many of them deeply unhelpful, which is why I had to ask her to leave. My fondest memory of Mo will be during the visit of our good friend, the Revd. William Clinton of the Church of the Seven Day Fornicators. While Bill and I were discussing important spiritual matters, Mrs Mowlam burst into my study waving a teapot shouting "I'm the new tea lady around here. Does anyone fancy a quick one?" And guess what? The Revd. Bill actually thought she meant something else! Which, knowing Mo, she probably did! Anyway, best wishes to Mrs Mowlam in whichever asylum she chooses to spend her remaining days! T.B

Millennium Tent Update
From P-Y Gerbil, Le Tent Supremo (ex)

Merde, alors! Quelle catastrophe! Le grand idiot milord Falconer, quel tosseur comme vous dites, a donné moi le "sack". Eh, pourquoi? No one, et je mean no one, pouvait faire un succes de cet miserable, useless tente! Un elephant blanc, si j'ever saw one! Naturellement, il etait un total floppe! Moi, j'accuse le milord Falconer, le "crony de Tony" comme vous dites. Il est le guilty homme. Sackez-lui, pas moi, pauvre petit Gerbil.

OK, j'ai perdu beacoup de millions de pounds donnés par le Parish lottery. Mais so what? Je ne regrette rien. Et, anyway, le tente est encore le meilleur value attraction touristique de tout le monde, beaucoup plus interessant que Buckingham Palace, whatever votre Prince Charles may have dit!

So, venez, venez, venez, pendant my job lasts.

P-Y. Gerbil

P.S. Nous regrettons que le tente est fermé, due to leaks dans le roof.

Putting The Record Straight

I understand that one of our parishioners, a Mr Rawnsley, has been spreading unpleasant and malicious rumours about an alleged "feud" between myself and our treasurer, my friend Mr Brown. I do not intend to dignify Mr Rawnsley's tittle-tattle by giving further currency to such stories as

- Mr Brown coming round to the vicarage in the middle of the night screaming abuse about the collection plate
- Mr Brown and our former churchwarden hitting each other with hassocks in the vestry after evensong
- me suggesting that Mr Brown was "some sort of lunatic who needed professional help".

All of these stories may be true, but nothing is gained by Mr Rawnsley going round repeating them. He should be ashamed of himself (as should Gordon and Peter!). T.B.

Special Brighton Outing Edition

Hullo!

And what a marvellous day out we all had in Brighton, despite the best efforts of some troublemakers who wanted to spoil our big day!

We were obviously very grateful to the police for arresting those silly farmers before they could make fools of themselves, and for baton-charging Mrs Mortimer and her friends from the St Albion's Hunt.

But otherwise our annual outing was a huge success and everybody was kind enough to say that my service on the beach was the best they had ever been to!

What made it particularly special for me was that Cherie and baby Leo were able to be with me, despite some people's prudish objections to Cherie breast-feeding during prayers!

I really would have hoped that in the 21st century we could have a slightly more grown-up and modern attitude to working babies and their mothers!

But of course I wasn't the only person who made our outing such a fantastic success.

Mr Prescott had everyone in fits of laughter with his amusing stand-up comedy routine at the end of the pier, and we were particularly amused by his hat which read "Kiss Quick Me" and his joke about what he'd like to do to the "stuck-up toffs" who like hunting!

You know, it's amazing that John, who started life as just a humble member of the working classes, is now able to take his place at the very centre of parish life, working under someone like me who has had so many privileges!

Well done, John! We're all very proud of you! And well done also, Mr Brown, our treasurer!

Some people may have thought that when Gordon gave us his little talk, he might have strayed rather too far from the subject of parish finances, which is what he was asked to talk about!

Still, for someone who is not known for his oratorical skills, he made a valiant effort not to be too boring, and the congregation very generously gave him a very supportive standing ovation!

Who says there's no charity at St Albion's!

A friendly word of warning to Gordon's new wife Sarah, however. Next year it might be advisable for her not to try to upstage the other ladies by wearing such a loud red dress! And by the way, Gordon, there's no need for you to copy Mr Gore, the American evangelist, by kissing your wife in public! Some things really should be done in private, even in this modern 21st century!

But that's enough of Gordon! Let's get back to that marvellous service, the edited highlights of which are reprinted overleaf in response to overwhelming public demand!

Enjoy!

Tony

We were delighted to welcome as our visiting preacher Rev. Mandela of the Free Nelson Mandela Church of South Africa. This was a great chance to meet one of the most important religious figures of our time – and Rev. Mandela was very grateful for the opportunity! A.C.

The Vicar's Brighton Service In Full – Edited Highlights

Confession

Vicar: Let's face it, we've had a few problems in the parish recently. And it would be dishonest of me not to admit it. The Millennium Tent has not gone quite as well as we hoped. And even though it was nothing to do with me, I'm prepared to accept responsibility for that.

The poor box. 75p for our old people. It's not good enough, is it? Gordon will have to do better.

Absolution

Vicar: But let's not dwell on the past. We must remember that most of the problems at St Albion's were the fault of my predecessor, the Rev. Major. Let's learn to forgive. So if one or two things have gone wrong in recent months, I forgive you all!

The Creed

Vicar: I believe passionately in an irreducible core of beliefs. And those beliefs make up my vision. And that vision is what I believe in. It's something I want you all to share. For without a vision, there can be no beliefs. And without belief, there can be no vision.

Commination

Vicar: Hey, anybody who thinks that young William Hague is fit to be the vicar when he grows up must be as drunk as William is every night down at the youth club.

But seriously. If you want me to be a racist, I just can't do it. If you want me to be a Satanist, then that's just not something I can do. If you want me to be a paedophile and a mass-murderer then, look, you can count me out. Young William is your man.

The Comforting Words

Vicar: I am listening. I hear. I act as though I care. Be of good faith for I am with you always. Now and for ever.

Peroration

Vicar: Life is a journey. And also a fight. A fight for what is right. A journey towards what is right. A fight for the right to a journey. A journey to a fight. And, God willing, it is a journey we will win.

Editor's Note: Those of us who were lucky enough to be there will never forget the rapturous applause which greeted these words, as the Vicar stood before us, his face bathed in an unearthly sweat. It was a miracle!

Parish Postbag...

Dear Sir,

May I through your columns thank all the parishioners who sent flowers, gifts and messages on my enforced retirement from the PCC. You have all been so kind and generous, and I only wish I could say the same of the vic

Yours gratefully
Mrs Mowlam ("Mo")
The Old Bus Shelter,
somewhere on the
High Street

The Editor: All letters from Mrs Mowlam may have to be cut for reasons of lunacy, inebriation or other infirmity.

✝ To Remember In Your Prayers

The people of Denmark who have made a very bad decision this week through ignorance, selfishness and their own deliberate fault. They have turned down the chance to belong to the Big European Family of Churches – the Ecumenical Union. Let us pray that their economy collapses, that there is rioting in the streets, that their bacon is infected with swine fever, and that their football team loses all its games. T.B.

St Albion's Women's Institute
NEWS

● Mrs Jay, Matron of the Old People's Home (the Rev. Callaghan's daughter!) gave a most interesting talk on country life. She told us that she knew a lot about the countryside because she had once seen it out of a train window on her way to London.

● Mrs Coote raised the question, "Does the Vicar really take women seriously?" The answer came from the Vicar's secretary, Mrs Anji Hunter, who offered the Vicar's apologies for his absence. "Of course Tony takes women seriously, but you can hardly expect him to come along in person just to listen to a lot of silly women airing their grievances."

ST ALBION PARISH NEWS

20th October 2000

Hullo!

And with the season of goodwill just around the corner, I've got two very important messages for the whole parish to take on board.

The first is very much for our younger parishioners. And I know how much kids today hate being preached at.

So let me assure them right away that this is not a sermon. It's just a piece of friendly advice, passed on from someone who may be a little bit older than you, but is still pretty "cool at heart". In fact you may be surprised to hear this, but your vicar once played lead guitar in a really wicked rock 'n' roll band back in his uni days.

And if you don't believe me, check out my website for this month's "Hot Vic Pic" at www.cooltony.com!

(Our band incidentally was called the Oxford University Popular Music Orchestra.)

Anyway, to get to the point. The parish really doesn't need any more single mothers. For a start, we simply can't afford it.

So that's why Yvette Cooper (or "Mrs Balls" as she is affectionately known!) will be giving a series of short talks at the beginning of the Youth Club's weekly disco night on the general message of "Avoiding Teenage Pregnancy".

Mrs Balls will be telling the girls to "Just say no." And I will be telling the boys, "It's OK guys, but for heaven's sake be sensible and wear a condom." In fact we're going to install a vending machine in the crypt, next to the coffee machine. So there's no excuse for any of you to find yourself in the family way!

Sermon over, OK?

Now, part two for the adults. Mr Straw of our Neighbourhood Watch and I have been putting our heads together to work out a way of getting rid of the beggars who give such a bad impression to visitors to St. Albion's.

Only recently there was a comment in the Visitors' Book "What a lovely church, but who are those ghastly young people lying in the porch in their sleeping bags?"

To be fair, on that occasion it was Euan and his schoolfriends. But point taken!

So let's stop encouraging these beggars by giving them money! Just say no! And, if you can't stop yourself, then for heaven's sake wear a condom! *Sermon over! OK?*

Do you remember the story in the Good Book about the Good Samaritan who saw this beggar lying by the side of the road?

He passed by on the other side of the road, which was the correct thing to do – leaving it to the professionals, such as the Samaritans, to sort it all out.

So the message is loud and clear. As it says in the book, if a man asks for bread, call the police and have him arrested!

That should be our message this Christmas!

Cheers!

Tony

Parish Bookstall

There are no copies of Mr Geoffrey Robinson's new book about himself on sale in the vestry. This is because there is no demand for it – as I keep telling all the hundreds of silly Parishioners who keep asking!!
T.B.

✝ To Remember In Your Prayers

● Mr and Mr Hinduja who gave so generously to support the Multi-Faith Zone in our Millennium Tent, but who now find themselves wanted by the police in their native India for alleged corruption. Let us all pray that these two gentlemen are extradited as soon as possible, to save St Albion's any further embarrassment!

● Also the late Mr Dewar who was a true Scotsman, a great parishioner and above all a friend of mine. T.B.

 ## Parish Postbag...

From Mr Alastair Campbell, Editor

Dear Myself,

The vicar's wife has asked me to make clear that she never spoke to Mr Branson at the Vicarage Cheese and Wine Party last year. Nor did they discuss who should run the Parish Tombola. And she certainly did not say to him, as some have alleged, "Don't worry, Richard. You've got it in the bag."

Yours sincerely,
A. Campbell

The Editor reserves the right to print all letters from himself in full.

Parish Tombola
An Announcement

■ I have had to ask Mr Burns, who used to look after the parish finances, to sort  this one out. This is, of course, no reflection on Chris Smith, who is responsible for this mess, nor his friend Mrs Shovelton, who we have just had to sack for her incompetence. However, I am sure Mr Burns will knock heads together, and that the Tombola will soon be run as efficiently as the Millennium Tent. T.B.

NOTICES

Mr Cook will be giving a talk with slides on his recent visit to the Holy Land and how he was able to bring the Muslims and the Jews together in a multi-faith stone-throwing competition. You are asked to come early, as no-one else will. A.C.

ST ALBION PARISH NEWS

3rd November 2000

Hullo!
And this week I've got something really important to talk about!
Saving the planet! And you can't get more important than that!
Which is why I dedicated last Sunday's family service to the
theme of "the environment". And my sermon was so popular that Mr
Campbell has asked me whether he can print it here instead of my
usual letter!

I said, "Of course, Alastair, a really cool idea! I'm all in favour of
re-cycling!" So, enjoy!

━ THE VICAR'S GREEN SERMON ━

*I would like to begin by welcoming you all to St Albion's on this
lovely autumn morning. You know, we hear a lot today about how
young people don't care about anything any more and have no
ideals.*

*Well, let me tell you a story about something which happened to
me last week. I came home one night to find my son Euan, with a
group of his schoolfriends, sitting around in the kitchen chatting
over a bottle of Smirnoff lemonade. And you know what they were
talking about? Let me tell you. One of them said "Euan's gone a bit
green," and another one said "Yes, very green, actually," and they
all agreed about how green Euan was. He, being a modest young
man, tried to play it down, but in the end he did admit to "feeling
terribly green" and he was so worked up about it that he had to go
to bed. And that set me thinking about the whole natural world and
how vital it is to us all – trees, plants, fish, animals, the lot! And we
are the custodians for all these wonders of nature!*

*We are just the steward while the master is away. And that is why
it is our duty to do everything we can.*

*Genetically modified tomatoes, global warming, the ozone layer,
the rain forests, wind farms, unleaded petrol. Aren't all these things
of enormous importance?*

*And that's why it's specially important that we should all think
about these things very carefully.*

*We need to take a long hard look at where we have come from and
where we are going! Because we are all coming from somewhere, and
we're all going somewhere else, whether we like it or not!*

There are hard choices to make. A field of wheat or an old
people's home? A hedgerow, or a new NHS hospital?
A sparrow on the wing, or a day care centre for toddlers?
These are the tough decisions we have to make! All of us!
So let's hear no more about easy options and "going green" just
for the sake of it!
That sort of argument may be alright when you're in the sixth
form. But when you're in the real world, you have to "get real"!
So, let's have a few seconds of silence to think about all these
important questions, before we sing our new chorus:

> *Green, green, green, green,*
> *We're the greenest greens you've ever seen,*
> *We all want to save the planet,*
> *Make it safe for John and Janet!*
> *Because we're green, green, green, green!*

© Words and Music T. Blair and J. Porrit.

Tony

✝ **To Remember In Your Prayers**

The Rev. Ashdown, the former minister
of the United Reformed Liberal
Democratic Church, who is still very
bitter about the failure of his attempt to
join our two congregations in an
oecumenical merger.

May he be given the strength to face
up to his own failure, not only as a
pastor but as a husband. Our prayers
go out to his wife Jane who has to face
the grim prospect of spending the rest
of her life with such an obvious
bounder. T.B.

Parish Notices

Women's Group

There was a very good turn-out for a talk by the Vicar's wife on "Modern Parenting – Aren't I Marvellous?".

Cherie began by accepting an award as "The Most Successful Mother In The Parish". She then told us that despite the difficulties of combining motherhood with a career, she always put her children first. We were all then very impressed when, after three minutes, her mobile phone went off and she was summoned to her office to meet a very important client, a lady, who is suing Southern Water because she thought her cup of tea tasted funny and she wanted £2 million compensation.

There was only time for one question from the floor, which was Mrs Harris, who asked, "Who is going to pick up the children from school?" "Tony, of course," came Cherie's reply, earning her a standing ovation. A.C.

A Big Thank You!

...to all of you who wrote in to say how moving you found my reading from the Book of Isaiah at Mr Dewar's funeral. Some of you obviously thought Mr Brown's address was a bit over the top, but I thought he did pretty well, considering that he's not a vicar (and is never likely to be!). T.B.

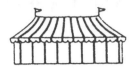

Millennium Tent Update

P-Y Gerbil writes:

Mesdames, messieurs,

Rollez-up pour le grand Ceremony de Closing du Tente Millennial sur Décembre 31. Dansez all nuit à la musique très groovy de la Ministère de Sound! Par coincidence amazing, un night-club owné par M. Palumbo, un grand ami de Mandelson, le "Ministère du Sound-Bite"! Nudge, nudge, wink, wink, comme vous Anglais disez! Entrée absolument libre au tente (fermé à 6pm). £75 pour le disco.

Une Amazing Nuit!
P-Y. Gerbil
Grand Supremo du Tente Millennial.

PS. Après janvier je serais available pour any poste importante, eg, le directeur de Railtrack ou sweeping les rues!

Ooh-la-la! Zere is nothing like a Dome!

ST ALBION PARISH NEWS

17th November 2000

Hullo!

And a very wet hullo it is too!

As I write the rain is still pouring down outside the vicarage window, as it has done every day for the past four weeks, and pretty well the whole parish is under water.

Even as I write, I can see Mr Prescott speeding past in one of his two powerboats, on his way to offer his sympathy to those who have had to retreat to the first floor of their homes thanks to the River Alb rising a record 27 metres (or do I mean 8 old feet?) in the past 24 hours.

I know it has not been easy for a lot of you, especially those of you living in the more low-lying parts of the parish, such as Flood Street, Burstbank Avenue and Sandbag Villas.

But, you know, the whole point of these sorts of disasters is to make us focus on the big questions.

Is this an Act of God? Or is it something we could have avoided? If the lorry drivers had used less fuel, then perhaps the climate wouldn't have changed, one could argue.

Or perhaps we should look on the floods as a blessing in disguise; in that when the streets are full of water, we can't use our cars?

Because, you know, these changes in the climate are a terrible warning of what may happen if we ruin the environment too much with our petrol fumes.

As our distinguished benefactor Prince Charles said last week in his talk to the St Albion's Green Society (what a pity so few of you could make it – I expect it was the floods), "you know, this whole sort of ozone layer, global organic thingie, is terribly worrying."

I am sure we could all benefit from thinking about what he said, particularly the lorry drivers who have been causing an obstruction outside Tesco's in the High Street, and swigging lager out of their Sun newspapers! Hey, no offence to the trucking community! But as Mr Prescott said, "Why don't they truck off?"

This seemed to make everyone laugh during the coffee after Sunday's evensong, and I must say Mr Prescott has been in his element lately (ie, water!), wading into everything with both feet, and finding himself up to his neck in the brown stuff (and I don't mean Gordon!)!

But let's not get too carried away by all this talk about global warming.

I mean, we have to accept that in the modern world everyone needs a car to get from A to B.

I mean, you can't rely on public transport these days. Look, we've all got to drive, which is why God has given us cars.

And, yes, we must do everything we can to protect our planet for the sake of our children and our grandchildren (not that I've got any, at least not that I know of!).

But it's only sensible to cut the price of petrol for the most vulnerable members of our community, such as pensioners, nurses and the owners of large haulage companies.

As it says in the Good Book, "for everything there is a season. A time to raise taxes, and a time to lower them" (*Book of Prudence, Ch. 14, v. 1*).

Yours still afloat!

Tony

Neighbourhood Watch with P.C. Straw

We have a growing problem in the parish with lorry drivers. We must all join together in cracking down on these trouble-makers before this problem gets out of hand. If you know of any lorry drivers, phone me in complete confidence telling me where they live, and their phone numbers. We must nip this menace in the bud before the toddlers and old folk of St Albion's are deprived of vital food and medical supplies.

J. Straw
Neighbourhood Watch
Co-Ordinator

Verses By A Local Poet

Water, water everywhere,
Just as the poet wrote,
But don't lose heart just
    yet, dear friends,
Here's Tony in his boat!
We may have lost our
    furniture,
Our lounge may smell just
    vile,
But now the vicar's here,
    dear friends,
To warm us with his smile!

M. Barg, runner-up in the
St Albion's Senior Citizen
Poetry Prize

Begging In The Parish – A Message From The Vicar

Just say Mo!

Some of you may recently have noticed a rather sad, scruffily-dressed lady, known as "Ow Mo", who stands in the High Street, talking to herself, and asking passengers-by for "some spare change". It is very important not to give her any because, whatever she pretends, she will only spend it on buying drink or cannabis. That is why it is particularly important this Christmas not to give money to people like Mo, for their own good. Leave it to the professional carers to deal with this problem. T.B.

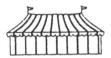

Millennium Tent Update
P-Y Gerbil writes:

Zut alors! Quel jour amazing! Non, mais vraiment! C'est juste comme une filme de James Bond, ou Topkapi avec Melina Mercouri – ooh-la-la, une amazing dame! Non, mais serieusement, trois cheers pour les hommes en bleu qui préventés le plus grand jewel heist en l'histoire de St Albion's! Un gang de thieves a planné de voler exhibit numéro un dans le Millennium Tent – Un Pair de Cufflinks en Imitation Diamond d'un grand value de £2.99 (kindly loaned par notre ami M. Ratner du magasin Crap 'R' Us dans le High Street). Mais heureusement, le theft etait un complete cock-up, juste like le tent!!

P-Y. J.

PS. Grande Conteste de Beauty on Samedi! Beaucoup de femmes voluptueuses dans leurs swimming costumes! Le Juge: Monsieur Chris Woodhead. Ne missez pas!

Parish Notices

The Vicar's talk on the **Importance of the Family** has been cancelled and he will be replaced by Mrs Jay (Rev. Callaghan's daughter) who will talk on the **Importance of Breaking Up Families** instead. A.C.

ST ALBION PARISH NEWS

1st December 2000

Hullo!

The nights are drawing in, and soon we shall be celebrating Christmas. But I have to confess that, as of now, I am finding it rather difficult to summon up any seasonal goodwill!

The former incumbent of this parish, Archdeaconess Thatcher, who was of course our first and only lady vicar, has seen fit to make a totally uncalled-for and hurtful attack on the way I am running the parish.

Look, I frankly have better things to do with my time than to answer the criticisms of every bitter old lady who is no longer in the limelight and can't bear it!

Hey, as it says in the Good Book, "Life is too short" *(Book of Platitudes, Ch. 14, v. 3)* to bother about the small-minded carping of someone who no one pays any attention to.

Very few of you probably even noticed what my predecessor said, when she stood up in the middle of evensong, waving her handbag and shouting at me.

She called me "vain" and "weak" and accused me of "monumental folly".

Pretty rude, you'll agree, not to mention totally untrue. In fact, there are probably some of you who would agree that I have every right to seek legal redress under the new Human Rights Act, which guarantees the right of every individual not to be vilified by deranged elderly women, who have probably had too much to drink at lunchtime! (Thanks, Cherie, for the free legal advice on that one!)

So, let's draw a line in the sand under the whole unpleasant business of the Rev. Thatcher, shall we? As Our Lord himself said, "Forgive and forget" *(Book of Cliches, 5.3)*.

But it's pretty difficult, isn't it, to forgive and forget, when it is someone whom you've really gone out of your way to be pleasant to; someone you've invited back to the vicarage to ask their advice; someone you've said nice things about in public; and then she turns round and makes these cruel and pointless remarks which, frankly, she should have kept her mouth shut about!

Goodness me, when I think of all the trouble we've been put to trying to sort out the mess she left of the parish after her eleven years in charge!

I don't want to go into it in detail, but let's just look at some of the things I am thinking of:

- no money spent on repairing church fabric for years on end
- selling off valuable church silver
- bringing in a private firm to run the flower roster
- introduced the ill-fated "sponsored pew scheme", giving preferential seating arrangements to local businesses
- imposing charges for after-service coffee and biscuits, which had previously been provided free to all worshippers, regardless of creed, colour, gender orientation or socio-economic status.

Frankly, I could fill up the whole of this newsletter with examples of the disastrous mismanagement of the parish during the years 1979-1990.

But obviously I am not going to waste space on all that. It is time to move on! Time to look forward and to accept that it is a different world out there! And, let's be fair, not everything the Rev. Thatcher did was bad. For example, I am thinking in particular of the considerable improvement in church finances made possible by the pew scheme, the coffee levy, the new "public-private" flower roster arrangements, etc, etc.

But none of this excuses her recent conduct in describing me as "useless". What a pity she sold off our local mental hospital to become the St Albion's Business Park, otherwise she would have been a prime candidate to be locked up there forever! (No offence, Margaret!).

Anyway, that's quite enough about the Rev. Thatcher in a week when I've got many more important things to write about!

Yours,

Tony

✝ **To Remember In Your Prayers**

- Poor Dennis Thatcher who, for so many years, has had to put up with living with a woman suffering from delusions. Let us not judge him for taking refuge in the bottle. Which one of us would not have done, if we were married to her? Amen.

⚝ NEW YEAR ⚝ FIREWORKS

■ There will be no fireworks display in the parish this year. Unfortunately, Mr Livingstone and his friend Mr Geldof did not think things through properly, so Mr Prescott has quite rightly refused to allow them to use the field behind the Working Men's Club (or anywhere else for that matter!) for reasons of health and safety. Sorry, Ken, but honestly it was a very stupid idea! T.B.

IMPORTANT CLARIFICATION

■ The Vicar's wife would like to make clear that when she attended the Diwali celebrations organised by the local Hindu community, it is simply untrue and highly defamatory to suggest that she was given a costly sari by Mr & Mr Hinduja – two local brothers with a fine reputation for supplying alms. It is true that Cherie wore the sari on a few occasions, but she subsequently donated it to the Parish bring-and-buy sale when people started to gossip, and it will now be used for the shepherds' robes in this year's Nativity Play.
Well done, Cherie!

Parish Postbag...

Dear Vicar
*   You stupid, fokking fokker!*
What sort of eedjit do you think
you
*   Yours sincerely*
*   R. Geldof*
*   Proprietor,*
*   Sparklers R Us,*
*   the High Street*
The Editor reserves the right to cut letters on grounds of obscenity. A.C.

Millennium Tent Update

P-Y Gerbil writes:

Bonjour! Et j'ai grandes nouvelles pour les "fans" de notre tente millenniaire! Enfin, nous avons trouvés un punteur pour acheter cette edifice magnifique! Et qui est-il, ce penteur extraordinaire? C'est moi, P-Y Gerbil, qui sera la proprietaire de la tente! Quelle amazing turn-up pour le libre, n'est-ce-pas? Alors, oubliez-vous le dot.com park de technology! Et bienvenu la grande Tente de Gerbil! Rollez, rollez up pour un Absolument Amazing Jour!!!
*   Votre ami, P-Y Gerbil.*

PS. Si vous avez des bonnes idées pour ma tente, ou l'argent pour l'acheter, donnez-moi un bell sur ma mobile (0777 330 338)!

Notices *Women's Group*

Why Women Aren't Being Given Their Share Of Top Jobs

Speaker, Mrs Margaret Jay (daughter of Rev. Callaghan), matron of the St Albion's Sunrise Old Folks Home, chair of the Parish Women's Committee, assistant convenor of the PCC steering group, adviser to the vicar on local media issues, co-chair Parish Family Outreach Action Group, etc, etc.

Hullo!

And a Happy Holiday Season to you all!

Like many of you, I have been out in the High Street amidst the bustling crowds as they make their preparations for the Big Day!

But, you know, there's always a small minority, isn't there, who try to ruin everything, with their mindless and thoughtless behaviour!

I'm thinking of what Mr Straw, the co-ordinator of our Neighbourhood Watch, recently described in a memorable phrase coined for him by Mr Campbell as "the yob culture".

We like to think of ourselves as tolerant people. But when we see the office parties spilling out onto the streets from the Britannia Arms, with their beer cans and their foul language, don't we all think it's time we became a lot more intolerant towards this kind of loutishness?

Only the other day, I was talking to one of our local taxi-drivers, who was driving Cherie and myself back from Mr Hinduja's Diwali Party at the St Albion's Trust Forte, and he said, "Vicar, do you know what I would do with these yobs? I'd string them up, because it is the only language they understand."

Strong language perhaps! But you know, my cab driver friend had a point!

It's all very well Cherie going on about human rights. But what about the rights of the ordinary people who are sick and tired of having their lives ruined by drunken, shaven-headed teenagers, who think it's clever to be able to down 14 pints in the course of an evening, and then go round shouting abuse at people like the Vicar.

So what it all comes down to, as Mr Straw told us at our recent Neighbourhood Watch Meeting, is that it is now time for action rather than words. Which is why, in the next few weeks, Mr Straw and I will be giving a whole series of talks around the parish, outlining the sort of measures which should be taken to stop these hooligans in their tracks.

The vital thing is that we should all be resolved to take the toughest and most drastic steps to crack down on every kind of criminal behaviour in our parish. And this is no longer something we can just leave to the police, since, for obvious reasons, there are very few of them left on the St Albion's beat.

The truth is that it is up to every one of us to play a part in this one.

We can no longer afford to tolerate what Mr Straw has called, in another memorable phrase, also suggested to him by Mr Campbell, the "walk-on by society".

That is why we need a real crackdown on all those people who believe in the walk-on-by ethic, which is what allows the yob culture to flourish.

It is the walk-on-by ethic which says "yes" to the lager lout, "yes" to the skinhead, "yes" to the drug pusher and the fox-hunters and all the other criminal elements who try to destroy the very fabric of our communal life here in St Albion's.

That is why I have written a special chorus for this year's St Albion's Carol Service, based loosely on a popular song from the Sixties:

> *When you see a lager lout*
> > *Drunk in the street*
> *Who shouts abuse*
> > *Whenever you meet.*
> *Don't walk on by,*
> > *Don't walk on by.*
>
> *If you see a hooligan*
> > *After he's had a couple of jars*
> *Wandering down the high street*
> > *And breaking into cars,*
> *Don't walk on by.*
> > *(But don't have a go either.*
> *Leave it to the police.*
> > *Even if there aren't any.)*

Words and music T. Blair

Do come along and join in the singing! Mulled wine will be served in the vestry afterwards (one glass only!).

Yours

Tony

Nativity Play

Mrs Jowell writes:

 There will be some changes to the traditional format of our Christmas story this year, to reflect the changing patterns of modern society, with particular regard to the family as a much more flexible and multi-faceted grouping.

We have therefore dropped the character of Joseph in the manger scene and replaced him with a female birth-partner, with whom Mary has chosen to share the experience.

The outmoded Holy Family thus becomes a more balanced two-women-and-one-baby unit, which relates more directly to the norms of contemporary society.

Millennium Tent Update

M'aidez, m'aidez, m'aidez from Le Grand Chef Supreme de la Tente Millenniaire, P-Y Gerbil.

Mes amis,

Je suis un grand personage maintenant, merci à tous les supplements et journaux qui a écrit millions de mots au sujet de moi-même, votres truly P-Y G. C'est tout very well pour le Vicaire, Monsieur Tony, de wash his hands de la tente, et pour Milord Falconer de rejecter mon bid pour le "takeover" de la tente, mais c'est moi qui a le support de tous les punteurs qui sont absolument over la lune après having enjoyed un Grand Jour Amazing dans ma tente!

Je veux à tous mes amis One Amazing Jour De Noel!
P-Y Gerbil.

PS. Nous avons maintenant un nouveau exhibit magnifique dans "Le Zone De Gerbil". C'est mon "Scrapbook Millenniaire" avec tous les millions de press cuttings au sujet de moi! Absolument libre à tous les punteurs! Mais vite, vite, vite, il y a seulement trois semaines jusqu'à la dernière Amazing Day!

From The Vicar
A Special Christmas Round Robin
To All Parishioners
(to be inserted inside the Vicar's Christmas Card)

Dear . . . .

I obviously don't have time to give you all an individual
Christmas message of goodwill and peace though I was lucky
enough to meet several of you at Mr Dimbleby's "Meet The Vicar"
Wine and Cheese Evening in the Carlton Hall. It was marvellous to
hear your concerns and I'm sorry I wasn't able to deal "in-depth"
with all your excellent questions. But Mr Dimbleby has kindly
suggested that we do it again soon. What a brilliant idea! Provided,
of course, the hall is available – which Mr Campbell says it isn't!

Well, what a year it's been and how quickly time has flown. The
big event at the vicarage has obviously been the arrival of little
Leo(!). I've been losing a lot more sleep over Leo than I have over
some of the silly squabbles in the parish this year! Honestly, having
a child really puts things in perspective – like Gordon's disloyalty,
Mr Dobson's dismal performance in the Panto (and, by the way,
what a good job Ken is doing – just as I always said he would), Mr
Robinson's disloyalty, the lorry drivers blocking the high street,
Mrs Mowlam's disloyalty, Mr Prescott making a fool of himself
during the floods, etc, etc. I could go on, but it's Christmas and we
are meant to be positive and forward-looking! So, I don't think
Cherie will mind me saying that she has had a marvellous year
expanding her human rights business and opening up a new suite of
offices over the carpet shop. And yet, despite her busy schedule,
she is always home in time to remind me to put Leo to bed.

Well done, Cherie! And well done, Euan, who has gone from
strength to strength ("Tenants Export to Tenants Extra", he tells me.
Whatever that means!) and he assures me he is working "flat out"
to get his AA levels!

So, that's all for now, except to remind you that the Millennium

Tent wasn't a terrific flop after all. I went last week to say goodbye to Mr Gerbil and to thank him for the tremendous job he has done.

He greeted me with a broad smile and said, "Thank God – you're the first visitor we've had all week."

Also, commiserations to Mr Branson who was so keen to take over the Tombola. I only wish Richard could have accepted with better grace the fact that we have to be very careful about the kind of people we allow to run important parish institutions like the Tombola. We can't just have any old cowboy! *(This is not a reference to Mr Branson. A.C.)*

Well, I'd better sign off and leave you with our Christmas Card and its great funny message by Mr John O'Farrell!

Tony

Cherie Christmas and A Nappy New Year!

P.S. Nice one, John!

Hullo!

And a very happy New Year to you all!

I write these words on what used to be called The Feast of the Epiphany, when we traditionally remember the story of the three rich men who came bearing gifts.

And it's particularly timely that we should think about that old story today. Because here we are, 2000 years later, and some people still haven't got the message – which is that rich men have a very important part to play in the project.

When those three very wise rich men turned up to present their gifts, were they pursued by hordes of reporters from the tabloids?

Were there hysterical headlines in the Bethlehem Star demanding to know the identity of these mystery donors?

Did people say "What's in it for Caspar, Melchior and Balthazar?"

No, they did not! The rich men of those days were rightfully honoured and respected for their contributions!

How sad it is then that in our own times, when members of our own parish community, like Mr Hamlyn or Mr Ondaajte or Mr Sainsbury, are generous enough to put £2 million into the collection plate, everyone at once mocks and sneers and questions their motives.

Isn't it possible, one has to ask, that some people might think so highly of everything I am trying to do for the parish that they might be prepared to express their appreciation in monetary terms?

And this is not the first time we have had to put up with this kind of carping and sniping, when some generous parishioners have been good enough to dig deep into their pockets for the good of the parish!

I am sure you will all remember the fuss about Mr Ecclestone and the adverts for his tobacconist's shop in the parish magazine.

And again, when Mr and Mr Hinduja so generously agreed to become sponsors of our hugely successful Millennium Tent (now closed), all some people could do was to go on about a supposedly free sari that they had given Cherie.

Honestly, you'd think we'd have developed a slightly more modern attitude to money by now. As it says in the New Labour Testament, "Money is the root of all goodness" *(St Paul Hamlyn's*

Letter To The Guardian, Ch. 8 v. £2 million).
Is it too far-fetched to imagine that in 2000 years we will no longer be singing carols about Caspar, Melchior and Balthazar but about the three wise men of our own time, Hamlyn, Ondaatje and Sainsbury! There's something to think about in the New Year!

Yours,

Tony

Mrs Cherie Booth writes:

On reading the above letter, I would like to make clear that my human rights have been seriously breached by the unfounded allegation that I accepted a free gift of a sari from a Mr Hinduja. It is true that such a garment was offered to me by the gentleman in question, but I only wore it once at a parish Multi-Faith Wine and Cheese. Immediately after that I presented it to our local Oxfam Shop. Any further repetition of this unwarranted and gravely damaging allegation will immediately become the subject of legal proceedings.

Lairg and Booth,
The High Street
('Human Writs R Us')
E-mail: www.quidsin.con

 # Millennium Tent Latest

Oui, c'est moi, P-Y Gerbil!

Je suis still here, despite tous les efforts du vicar et son "cronies", comme M. Falconer, de flogger-off le tente à un autre ami, M. Bourne. Quelle scandale énorme, n'est-ce pas? M. Bourne est un ami de M. Mandelson (assez dit!) et il seulement wishes d'acheter le tente pour building hundreds de petits maisons pour les executives behind le vicarage.

C'est un disgrace. Tout le monde knows que le tente est un grand succes, thanks à moi et mon team, et should continuer pour un 1000 years sous le direction de votre reliable ami, P-Y G. (One Amazing Gerbil!).

Note from The Editor: Mr Gerbil has been under a lot of strain recently trying to run a hopelessly misconceived project which he has made even worse by his ineptitude. We naturally wish him well in his early retirement. A.C.

Parish In-Box

Dear Sir,

I was frankly appalled by the Vicar's Christmas card, which you reproduced in your last issue, showing the Vicar as the Madonna. I am usually open-minded on such matters, but this was disgus

Yours
(Name and address withheld)

(The editor reserves the right to censor all letters for reasons of space. A.C.)

HAPPY BIRTHDAY!

HAPPY BIRTHDAY to our own Mr Mandelson who was given a lovely party by Mr Bourne, one of the selfless rich men that I have been talking about so much recently.

Mr Bourne gave Peter a super time and, talking of giving generously, I have decided to give the Millennium Tent to Mr Bourne for almost nothing!

You see – it's catching, this "giving" business! T.B.

ANNOUNCEMENTS

■ Mr Prescott is delighted to announce that he has agreed to allow a new dual carriageway to be built through the fields behind the vicarage. There have been complaints from parishioners that Mr Prescott promised that he would stop this road but John has promised that we will hear no more about this. "There'll be too much noise from the bloody road," he says.

St Albion's School

Mr Blunkett, the Chairman of the Governors, would like to assure parents that there are no shortages of teachers in the school this term. There are plenty of teachers to cope with a full curriculum as normal. Term will begin slightly later than usual on Feb 22nd, with half-term commencing on Feb 23rd. More revised dates will be announced in due course.

● NEW TO THE PARISH ●

A big welcome to our new parishioner Mr Desmond, who has recently bought our local newsagents, now called "Dirty Des".

When we invited him to the vicarage for a mince pie, we were charmed! Some people might have been shocked by some of Mr Desmond's more colourful language, and by his offer to take pictures of Cherie in the nude for his new magazine Vicars' Wives! But I think we have to move with the times and, as a vicar, my job is to mix with people from every walk of life, and not be judgemental about it! T.B.

ST ALBION PARISH NEWS

26th January 2001

Hullo!

I want to share with you all this week my feeling of frustration at the way some people have chosen to misrepresent my non-appearance at the meeting in the Church Hall last week to debate the pros and cons of fox-hunting.

Some of the more unChristian parishioners have even accused me of cowardice, as if I were a fox running away from Mrs Mallalieu and her ladies who had gathered on horseback outside the hall!

Well, really! Look, let's get my position on this quite clear. It was me who organised the meeting. It was me who insisted that everyone should turn up.

And it was me who made it absolutely clear that in this modern age there was no place at all for a totally barbaric and cruel so-called sport like fox-hunting.

And in that sense it is easily the most important moral issue confronting our society today.

So, why wasn't I at the meeting, you may ask? The answer is very simple!

As the Vicar, I have a very busy diary, and hundreds of things to do on behalf of the parish. And I can't be in two places at once, much as I would often like to be!

The truth is that, after I had arranged last week's meeting, Mr Campbell reminded me that I had a very important and long-standing commitment in Belfast which I simply could not get out of.

There is nothing I would have liked more than to be with you all at the meeting on Wednesday, and even listening to Mrs Mortimer shouting "bastard" at me as I entered the hall!

But let's be honest. When it comes to priorities, the welfare of a few foxes doesn't exactly compare with the need to sort out the problems we've been having with our Mission to Northern Ireland.

That's why it was absolutely vital that I should fly over to have dinner with Mr Mandelson on Wednesday night, rather than have rotten tomatoes thrown at me outside the Church Hall by a lot of lunatic women on a cold night in January!

I was thus able to hear at first-hand just what a superb job I had done in appointing Peter to run the Mission! The Mission Hall has only been burned down twice since Christmas, which marks a real step forward in achieving our ambition to bring people together!

I was able to tell Peter this myself, on behalf of all of you, over a lovely dinner of salsa beans and guacamole chiquitos, beautifully prepared by Peter's partner Renaldo!

So, let's not have any more of this talk of me running away from my responsibilities on this frankly fairly minor issue of fox-hunting, which people keep going on about as if it was the only thing in the world which mattered!

I will organise as many meetings on the need to ban hunting as people in the parish want. But you can't expect me to attend any of them!

Now what could be braver than that?

Tally ho!

Tony

A Hymn For Septuagesima

Little foxy, little foxy,
With your bushy tail,
Keep on running, keep on
                    running,
Over hill and dale.
Little foxy, little foxy,
Hiding in your lair,
Don't you worry, don't you worry,
Here comes the Reverend Blair!

Words and music
T. Blair 2001.

A Statement From Mr Mandelson

There is no link between Mr Gobby Hinduja's generous donation to the Millennium Tent and the letter from my secretary asking the Vicar to sign his passport application.

I was not involved in any way and merely told Mr Hinduja that I would see what could be done on his behalf.

I would have provided this small act of charity to any other member of the parish who had offered me a million pounds.

P.M.

✠ To Remember In Your Prayers

■ Ms Germaine Greer, who has sent a rude e-mail round the parish accusing the Vicar's wife of acting like a "concubine" by attending the bring-and-buy sale and other parish functions. Give her strength to remember in a quiet moment of reflection that she herself may be, in a very real sense, a sour, bitter and twisted old witch who is nobody's concubine, let alone their wife! T.B.

St Albion's Hospice

Mr Milburn writes:

I have had a number of letters from parishioners complaining that their deceased loved ones have been found piled up in a broom cupboard. As the Vicar rightly says, this is not our fault and the people in charge should be ashamed of themselves.

A.M.

Pre-Lent Workshop

The Importance of Marriage
(held at Mrs Bourne's house on January 17)

The Vicar led the discussion by saying that marriage was very important in this day and age, and studies had shown that this was definitely the best way to bring up children.

Mrs Blair said she agreed, so long as both partners shared the responsibilities of parenting and housework, particularly if the wife had a more important job than the husband!

Mr Cook agreed, but pointed out that divorce was also a good thing, because you couldn't necessarily get it right the first time around, as Mrs Dewar had found out when she became Mrs Lairg.

Mr Smith and his partner then pointed out stable same-sex relationships were often better than straight marriages, too many of which ended in divorce, like Mr Straw's, Mr Milburn's and several other members of the PCC.

Mrs Jay then made a passionate speech in support of having relationships with other people's husbands, saying they were equally valid in their own way, and could lead to a permanent, loving and fulfilling relationship which could last for several years.

The Vicar summed up by saying that it had been a very thought-provoking evening, and that he felt many people's long-held views had been challenged by what they had heard. He thanked everyone for coming, and particularly Mrs Bourne for serving a delicious tea of smoked salmon sandwiches and champagne.

ST ALBION PARISH NEWS

9th February 2001

Hullo,

And a very sad "hullo" it is too, because of the tragic departure from the PCC of one of my dearest and best-loved friends, Mr Mandelson.

There is no need to go into the reasons for Peter's decision to submit his resignation when I asked for it.

As he is the first not to admit, he made a terrible mistake over the signing of Mr Hinduja's passport application form, having previously accepted Mr Hinduja's very generous donation of £1 million to our Millennium Tent fund.

But let none of us be too hard on Peter. He has been under terrible stress for some months now, and his mind may not always have been fully focussed on his parish duties, such as the running of our Mission to St Gerry's in Northern Ireland.

As Mr Campbell so charitably put it, "Poor Peter has become a little bit, how can I say, bonkers".

And that is why it is best for Peter to get right away from parish business, and perhaps the parish as well, and try to carve out some sort of meaningful new life for himself, a long way away. Perhaps Brazil would be a suitable place for him and his devoted partner Renaldo, where the tempo of life is more relaxed (and house prices are rather lower!)

I know some people in the parish have been asking, "How on earth will the Vicar manage without his former Churchwarden Peter beside him, to tell him what to do and what to say?"

Well, let me tell you, this is a little bit offensive to your Vicar, as you can well imagine! The implication is that I haven't got a mind of my own!

Well, I am sure Mr Campbell would have something pretty scathing to say about that, probably throwing a few salty words of the kind we try not to use at Evensong! *(Alastair, please don't cut this bit out!)*

So, let's forgive and forget about this one, shall we (and I mean particularly "forget"!). It's time to move on, and draw "a line in the sand under this one" as my predecessor the Revd. Mr Major was so fond of saying every time a member of his PCC was found in the organ loft with one of the ladies from the flower roster!

But, may I say, before I leave this subject, how personally

saddened I was by the response of some members of the PCC when I had to tell them the terrible news that Peter was leaving us.

Instead of looking suitably despondent, there was general merriment, including laughter, singing and, I understand, a reconvening of the meeting in the Britannia Arms that evening, when the entire stock of champagne in the pub cellar was drunk, to the chanting of "*'ere 'e goes, 'ere 'e goes, 'ere 'e goes*".

I sincerely hope that all those involved in these disgraceful scenes are now feeling suitably ashamed of themselves! I will not embarrass any of them by naming names, but the following may be only too aware who I have in mind: Mr Straw, Mr Brown, Mr Prescott, Mr Blunkett, Mr Byers, Miss Short, and indeed everyone else in the parish.

Yours regretfully,

Tony

Kids' Korner

The Gospel for the Young
(as told by the Vicar!)

THE STORY OF PETER THE FISHYMAN

Our Lord's favourite disciple was called Peter. Our Lord was very fond of him because he had helped him in his mission to spread the Good News. But, unfortunately, Peter (which is the Latin for "rocky") turned out to have serious psychological flaws. And when the testing time came, he let the Vicar down very badly. We call this the story of "Peter's Betrayal". As it says in the Good Book, "You are called Peter, for you are the rock on which my project might well founder."

Letter of Peter to the Sunday Times, 7.3 *(New Labour Bible)*

Parish Postbag

Dear Sir,

I was utterly disgusted and shocked by your appalling treatment of my good friend, Peter. You have behaved in a totally despicable, contemptible and utterly

Yours sincerely,
Robert Harris,
The Bunker, Berchtes Gardens.

The Editor reserves the right to cut all creepy, snivelling letters clearly dictated by Mr Mandelson to his only friend left in the world for reasons of space.

Dear Sir,

We represent Mr Peter Mandelson, whom we understand previously occupied the post of Churchwarden and Missioner to the Parish of St Albion's. We are instructed by our client to inform all parish newsletters that any allegations of lying, duplicity, mendaciousness or any other form of contumelious conduct whatsoever, will be met with the strongest possible response. We shall not hesitate to institute proceedings and to seek full legal redress.

Yours etc,
Gold-diggers & Co, Solicitors and
Commissioners of Shirts, Jermyn Street, London.

Thought for the Week

"Greater love hath no man than this, that he lay down his friend for his own life."

(Proverbs 7. 4)

Welcome. . .

...to Mr Reid, who has taken over the Mission to St Gerry's at short notice. And of course we also welcome his partner, Renalda, who is a well-known film-producer and director of that classic video Brazilian Dentist On The Job (available from Dirty Des, the vids 'n' mags shop run by Mr Desmond). I am sure parishioners will have seen this one in the privacy of their own houses! T.B.

Tidings From The Creche

We've had a terrific response to our Under 5s drawing competition to come up with a picture of the Vicar to go on his new letterhead. The drawing we all liked best was this one by Charlotte Millbank (aged 3½).

Says Charlotte: "It shows a big heart because the Vicar is all heart and a pair of legs because the Vicar has got plenty of legs and will go on being a successful vicar for years to come. Hooray for Tony."

And thanks to Alastair for taking down Charlotte's words so faithfully.

ST ALBION PARISH NEWS

Hullo!

Well, there's one person you certainly won't be reading about in my newsletter this week, and that's Mr Mandelson (or Peter, as he used to be known in happier days).

I think we've all heard quite enough about that gentleman for a lifetime, so I can assure you I won't be wasting any more time worrying about him and his sad mental decline!

Let's not mince words about this, shall we? Poor Peter has gone mad, and we all have a duty to do what we can to ignore him.

Personally, I was more than prepared to forgive him for being sacked, and to overlook his many acts of disloyalty and dishonesty over the years, had it not been for his truly disgraceful behaviour at our recent Diocesan "Mission 2001" launch.

Everyone had been looking forward to my major address outlining all our exciting new plans for the parish over the next 10 years.

I had spent a lot of time working on what I was going to say – I don't just make these things up on the spur of the moment, you know! – and I was going to explain in detail my thinking on how we could really deliver on all our promises to make the parish a more vibrant, inclusive, transparent and, let's face it, fun place to be. And what happened? No sooner had I begun speaking than there was this disturbance outside.

There was shouting, rude words, stones being thrown at the windows, and an unpleasant chant of "Vicar, vicar, vicar, out, out, out", led by none other than our poor, sad, demented former Churchwarden.

Although I attempted to continue valiantly with my talk, I could tell that the attention of the audience had been distracted by the noise outside.

And over coffee and biscuits afterwards (thank you to Mrs Brown for the organic oatmeal cookies!), all the talk was of "mad Mandy" and what an appalling example he set to the young people by his melo-dramatic tantrums.

I do not wish in any way to prejudge the impartial investigation which is being carried out by my good friend Mr Hammond into Mr Mandelson's behaviour.

It will be entirely up to him to decide one way or another that Mr Mandelson was guilty of all the things we said he was.

But, until then, we ought all of us to remember the words of Our Lord, "Let he who is without, let him not cast stones at those who are still within" *(Letter of St Antony to the Mandelsonians)*.

So, let's hear no more about Mr Mandelsonian in this newsletter or anywhere else!

We've got a future to build, and we've all got to play our part (except for you, Peter, obviously!).

Yours,

Tony

Stranger Danger!

Watch out for this man seen loitering around the village scrounging food and interviews.

DO NOT APPROACH HIM!

Issued by Mr Straw of the Neighbourhood Watch on behalf of the vicar.

Parish Postbag

Dear Sir,

May I, through your columns, give a very warm and heartfelt thank you to all those parishioners who sent me such lovely cards, cakes, flowers and, in one case, a beautiful hand-knitted fluffy jumper which I
Yours sincerely,
P. Mandelson, former Churchwarden
(and hopefully European
representative of the PCC!),
Hinduja Mansions, Notting Hill Road.

The Editor reserves the right to cut all letters from the traitor Mr Mandelson for reasons which must be obvious to anyone except Mr Harris! A.C.

Women's Groups

Our thanks to Mrs Jay, who made time in her very busy and successful life to give yet another interesting and useful talk on "Women and the Job Market".

Mrs Jay began by saying that women were at a clear disadvantage because they were not men! But there were all sorts of ways a woman could get round this and find a job. One was to buy the local paper and look under the "Jobs Vacant" section. Another was to go to the local Job Centre and ask whether they had anything available. But the best way of all, Mrs Jay said, was to make sure you had the right father, the right husband and the right friends, ie the Vicar!

Mrs Jowell, in the chair, thanked Mrs Jay for her very helpful and entertaining address, and said that from now on there could certainly be no excuse for any woman to be out of a job!

Editor's Note

As we go to press, we learn the sad news that Mrs Jay has decided to give up her job at the Old People's Home.

She tells us "I have enjoyed working for the Vicar very much. But I would like to have had a little more support from some of my male colleagues on the PCC. If I may say so, I think I did a good job. But now the time has come to spend more time telling my family what to do."

Fundraising Cheese and Wine Party

Mr. Lairg cordially invites all lawyers to a special
"Support the Vicar" Cheese and Wine Party
to be held in his office on
February 28th (Cash Wednesday).

Bring a bottle and at least £200.

Says Mr. Lairg "This is a real chance
to help the Vicar – and the Vicar
always remembers his friends in
all kinds of ways.
As it says in the Good Book
'A nudge for a nudge, and a wink for a wink.'

1 MILLENNIUM TENT
(not very much used)

Complete with pegs, guy ropes and almost life-size
papier-mâché model of the Vicar.
We will pay *you* to take it away!!!
All offers considered, except from P-Y. Gerbil,
especially from bona fide friends of the Vicar.
Would make perfect office block/housing
development/outdoor disco.

WORTH MILLIONS TO RIGHT OWNER
(*not* P-Y. Gerbil)
Genuine offers only, no time-wasters (That's you, M. Gerbil!)
Purchaser collects, bring own lorry.
Apply Mr Falconer, C/o The Vicarage.

ST ALBION PARISH NEWS

9th March 2001

Hullo!

Lent is upon us yet again, and I'm sure we're all thinking "What can I give up?"

With this thought in mind, can I tell you about a visit I recently made to our local prison, Thirdways, where I was able to talk one-on-one with some of the inmates.

And a very humbling experience it was!

After all, these are all people who in a very real sense have given up something very precious – their freedom on behalf of the community.

And the good news is that Mr Straw, who runs our Neighbour-hood Watch, has plenty of plans to enable more and more people to join them!

But that experience set me thinking. As I came out of the prison, I thought of all the other people in the community who could well benefit from a short time behind bars!

I don't want to name names, but our former churchwarden, Mr Mandelson, is one which immediately comes to mind!

And another, of course, is Mr Woodhead, who used to help out with the St Albion's sixth form (particularly, I have to say, certain of the girls!). It seems that he, like Mr Mandelson, is very bitter at no longer being part of the St Albion's team!

And then, of course, there are all the farmers who are asking for money because of this foot and mouth disease.

Surely they should be thinking seriously about why this should have happened to them? Might God not perhaps be trying to tell them something?

Something about all the terrible things they have done to the countryside in the pursuit of profit? Some of them making up to two thousand pounds a year!

After all, don't we read in the Good Book about how God would punish people in the older days? We remember the story about the Nazarene swine who got foot and mouth disease, so that Jesus, quite rightly, had to order them to jump over a cliff!

So, let's not hear any more whingeing from these farmers! Or else we'll all give up meat from Lent, and then see how they feel!

Not a bad idea actually, especially since when I was in Tesco's yesterday there was very little meat to be had, apart from some frankfurters marked "produce of Schweinenfever, Germany".

I was only sorry that my visit to Tesco's was once again ruined by our combative friend in the checkout queue, who shouted "I hope you're giving up for Lent, vicar!"

I had no idea what he meant, but said that I would be very pleased to visit him in Thirdways when he finds himself locked away there, which, in my view, is likely to happen in the very near future!

Yours,

Tony

The Vicar pays a visit to the St Alblon's Rehabilitation Centre for Drug Abusers and Down-and-Outs. He found time to meet Mr Booze who told us afterwards, "The Vicar seemed genuinely concerned that I had smoked pot in the vicarage and said he would alert the relevant authorities, especially the police."

EDITOR'S NOTE

In our next edition we shall be publishing selected extracts from Mr Hammond's report on the unfortunate resignation of our former churchwarden, Mr Mandelson. I, of course, haven't seen his report, the contents of which are strictly embargoed, but, from my reading of it, I'm afraid Mr Mandelson doesn't come out of it very well at all! A.C.

Lenten Addresses

The first of our series of Lent talks was given by Mr Straw of the Neighbourhood Watch. He took as his theme "The Deadly Sin of Greed", with particular reference to the legal profession. Mr Straw drew on his personal experience as a former lawyer to give us a fascinating insight into the absurd sums of money that lawyers can earn. Unfortunately, certain members of the audience, including the Vicar's wife and Mr Lairg, had to leave early after one minute, due to a sudden attack of 'flu.

In the discussion afterwards, Mr Vaz was warmly applauded when he pointed out that there was no need for lawyers to earn a lot of money from the law, because there were much easier ways to make a fortune.

Mrs Mortimer unfortunately introduced a sour note by saying that, although her husband was a very rich lawyer, she wasn't going to make any further donations to church funds, because the vicar had preached a sermon on "The Evils of Foxhunting". Our special thanks to Mrs Jowell for the delicious Organic GM Pancakes, supplied by Mr Sainsbury. Their unusual fishy flavour was much appreciated!

Announcement

I gather that the protest meeting scheduled to take place outside the Vicarage (the so-called "March Against The Vicar") has been postponed indefinitely. Good to see that people are giving up something sensible for Lent! T.B.

(PS. Thanks for the very funny joke, Mr O'Farrell!)

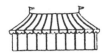

GRAND MILLENNIUM TENT AUCTION
by Mr Falconer

Many thanks to everyone who turned up to our very successful sale of the contents of the Millennium Tent. Among the lots sold were:

1 Giant Papier-Mache Gerbil (over 64 centimetres high) 12p

5 "Millennium Tent 2000" pens, inscribed "One Amazing Biro" 16p

1 Chemical Toilet (unused) in mint condition £1.20 *(This was a very good bargain for Mr Bragg!)*

1 Playstation II (easily repairable) from the "Forward To The Future Zone" 35p

1 packet frozen "Millenniburgers" (best before 31 December 2000) 5p

The grand total raised for Parish funds from the sale was £7.68. Well done, everyone!

ST ALBION PARISH NEWS

24th March 2001

Hullo,

And a special hullo to all of you who have written to me in recent months (and e-mailed me!) sharing your worries about the odd thing or two which may have gone wrong in the parish.

Not that I for a moment accept that anything serious is going wrong with the parish. And, honestly, from the tone of some of your letters, you would think that the world was coming to an end and that the Four Horsemen (or Horsepersons! Thanks, Cherie) of the Apocalypse were roaming across the land spreading destruction in their wake.

Not of course that they would be allowed to roam around St Albion's at the moment, thanks to the ban on movement around the parish imposed by Mr Nick Brown as part of his very sensible measures to protect us all from the farmers!

Look, let's face it, it's easy to get the impression that things are going wrong, when we see a lot of rather sensational stories in the papers about cows burning, trains crashing, old ladies lying on trolleys in hospital corridors, toddlers being sent home from school because their teachers are on strike, and the police failing to catch any criminals.

But, you know, this is not the real story of what is happening in our parish, is it? As you look around your own sitting room, do you see any old folk being left to die on trolleys?

As you look around your garden do you see any trains crashing or cows burning?

Of course not! Let's get these things in perspective, shall we?

The parish is doing fantastically well! As we saw last week, when Mr Brown presented our latest accounts, we've got more money in the bank than ever before (well done, Gordon, for putting some of my ideas into practice at last!).

Everyone has got jobs, class sizes at St Albion's Primary School are down to record levels (well done, Mr Blunkett!) and the waiting list at our Cottage Hospital has been cut to only 10 years. Not a bad set of achievements, is it?

Hey, this is a record anyone could be proud of! So the kind person who keeps sending me a text-message on my mobile saying "UR NBG VCR BGGR OFF!" should eat his abbreviated words. (Thanks for the joke, Mr O'Farrell!)

And that's also why, whatever the gloom-and-doom merchants may say, I have no intention of postponing this year's very important PCC elections, just because one or two disaffected people from outlying parts of the parish can't get in to vote (or do I mean "disinfected people"? – another cracker from Mr O'Farrell, St Albion's official new "Joker Laureate"!)

The point is that May is a very special month for me and Cherie. It is the month when you chose me as your vicar in 1997.

May is the month when Cherie chose to give the parish little Leo!

And don't let's forget that May 1st (or is 3rd?) is New Labour Day, when we celebrate the birth of the new and the death of the old by dancing round the maypole!

In fact, I have written a special chorus to be sung at Evensong called "The May Poll":

> *What a wonderful month is May!*
> *When you all can have your say!*
> *Take up your cross!*
> *Put it down by "the boss"!*
> *And hip, hip, hip, hooray! (Repeat)*

© Words and music T. Blair.

Yours,

Tony

Rambling Club
Round And About The Parish
With Mick Meacher

The days are lengthening, Spring is in the air and the crocuses and daffodils are showing their welcome little heads above the ground. Time, you think, to get out into the country and enjoy a good walk! I couldn't agree more, and that's why, even though there are a few minor restrictions just at present, there is no reason for us all to stay moping at home!

Here is my recommended *"Ramble of the Week"*, drawn up with the help of the AA and MAFF.

1. Walk from your house to your car, enjoying the view.
2. Drive to assembly point – Junction 29 (clockwise) of the M94 – to meet up with fellow ramblers.
3. Drive off round M94, appreciating breathtaking view of animals being burnt out of window.
4. 1300-1400 hrs. Meet for lunch at Little Chef by Junction 71. There will be an opportunity to buy souvenirs of the countryside from the Q8 minimart at Oondatje service station.
5. Complete tour of M94, enjoying further views of country life, farmers hanging themselves, etc.
6. 1630-1700 hrs. Tea break at the "Old McDonald's Drive-Thru" (Junction 106).
7. Drive home, and enjoy bracing walk from garage to living room (not forgetting to dip feet in disinfectant bath on the way!).

What You Should Take With You

Stout pair of driving shoes
Warm gloves
Copy of Sunday Telegraph to read in traffic jams.

Happy Rambling! **Mike Meacher**

 # Parish Postbag

Dear Sir,

Could I use your columns to express my profound thanks to my good friend Mr Hammond for so comprehensively clearing my name over the signing of Mr Hinduja's passport form.

As I have said all along, I did nothing wrong, but in no way do I feel any resentment towards my old friend the Vicar for having so understandably sacked me for doing nothing wrong, and I look forward to him keeping his side of the bargain after the PCC elections!

Peter Mandelson, Hinduja Mansions, Notting Hill Grove.

PS. Make sure this letter goes in in full, Alastair, or your days are numbered! P.M.

ST ALBION PARISH NEWS

Hi, everyone,

I hope you've all been enjoying your hot cross buns and your Easter bunnies!

Well, let me tell you, your Vicar is one very hot and cross bunny indeed at the moment. (Thanks to Mr O'Farrell for that one!)

But, seriously, I'm going to have to read the riot act this week over the way some people have been treating Mr Vaz (or Keith, as he is known to his good friends in the parish). No wonder he has been taken ill and I hope you are all ashamed of yourselves.

Keith, as you know, has made an absolutely invaluable contribution to the life of the parish in so many ways.

Let's not forget that he was the first Indian member of the PCC. (Shame on us for taking so long!) And what a positive signal that sent out, showing everyone that, when it comes to making parish appointments, we choose people irrespective of race, colour, creed or ability!

But certain people can't seem to be able to find it in their hearts to welcome people from other climes into our community on equal terms!

Goodness me, the stories that are being put around about Mr Vaz! If you believed half of them, you'd think that Keith had done something wrong.

For instance, it has been claimed that he was seen taking money out of the collection plate and putting it in his own pocket during the Offertory hymn, when everyone was busy singing "What a friend we have in Tony".

Can I just make it clear that there is absolutely no record of this at all! I personally arranged for Mrs Filkins to carry out a full investigation of all these charges against Keith.

And although, sadly, he was too busy on parish business down at the passport ofice to see her himself, Mrs Filkins nevertheless came to exactly the same conclusion as I had already done – that Keith, just like Peter before him, was innocent of any charge.

Well done, Mrs Filkins and your good ladies! So, let's have no more silly, hurtful tittle-tattle about Keith, shall we?

Instead, I'd like to take this opportunity to remember all the good things he has done for the parish since he joined our team.

Unfortunately, there isn't space to list all his many achievements.

But one stands out in particular.

And that was the selfless help he gave to local businessmen like the Hinduja brothers (Gotricha, Bakhanda and Boforsguna) who were having trouble with their passport applications.

Keith could not have done more to guide them through all the difficulties of filling in their forms, and he even asked me personally to put my signature on the back of their photographs.

And didn't it turn out well! The good brothers were so grateful that they quite coincidentally sent a very generous cheque for our Millennium Tent Appeal, which helped to make it such a huge success!

So, I would just liked to end by recording my complete faith in Mr Vaz and expressing my very deep personal sadness at the news, which he has yet to hear, that he will have to stand down after next month's PCC elections, in order to spend more time with his family.

Yours,

Tony

Upcoming Parish Dates

St Albion's Voodoo Society

■ Mr Reinaldo da Silva (Mr Mandelson's partner) will give a short talk on how to bring a curse on your enemies with the aid of a strangled chicken. Parishioners are warned **not** to try this one at home except under proper supervision by a qualified witch doctor. Admission free.

A New Easter Hymn

There is a green hill far away
Beyond the city wall.
So go out now and visit it,
But stay in your
car, that's all!

Words and music by "Ramblin' Mike" Meacher 2001

An Official Warning from Mr Byers, PCC Business Liaison Officer

ANYONE who bought copies of a book called *The Paymaster* by Tom Bower at last week's Bring-and-Buy sale may have committed a criminal offence.

They must at all costs return the book to me without reading it, or face prosecution. S.B.

Kids Corner

This picture (taken a few years ago!) shows a well-known parish personality when he was a student at a well-known university!

Is it a) Donny Osmond; b) David Cassidy; c) one of the Monkees; d) Rev. A.R.P. Blair MA (Oxon)?

A prize of the Millennium Tent (plus fridge, slightly rusty) will go to the first correct entry opened.

 ## Parish Postbag

Dear Sir,

I would just like to thank everyone who organised the recent party to celebrate my retirement after more than 50 years' service to the parish.

I look back on many happy times under previous incumbents, but I am only sorry that, since the arrival of the present Vicar, with his

Yours fraternally,
Tony Benn, The Old Teabag,
Tetley Road, PGT 1PS

The Editor reserves the right to cut all letters due to foot-and-mouth restrictions. A.C.

MILLENNIUM TENT

SPECIAL OFFER

STILL FOR SALE at a giveaway price (0p), this unique memento of our parish millennium celebrations still has not found a good home! Couldn't some kind person please offer to take the tent off our hands? It is currently becoming a bit of an eyesore, since various parishioners decided to use it as a dump

 and someone has thrown an old fridge on top of it. All offers gratefully accepted (except, of course, from P-Y Gerbil who made such a mess of our otherwise successful tent project!). T.B.

ST ALBION PARISH NEWS

20th April 2001

 Hullo!
I hope you all had a wonderful Easter, getting out into the country and spending lots of money in gift shops, rural craft museums and similar attractions.

What a wonderful reminder it was of how many glorious opportunities there are to spend your money in all our unique British countryside facilities.

And how ridiculous it is to imagine that there is nothing to see in the country except a lot of animals on fire. (Surely "on farms"? A.C.)

Why on earth, one can't help wondering, do people spend a fortune flying off for their holidays to places like Tuscany and the Seychelles when they could stay at home to visit such exciting tourist centres as the St Albion's Miniature Railway (temporarily closed due to the Easter Holiday track maintenance programme), the historic Martello Tower (closed due to cliff erosion) or our local Moth Sanctuary (closed due to Foot and Mouth).

So many of you were obviously out-and-about enjoying the pleasures of supporting the rural economy, that you did not make it to our special Multi-Denominational Easter, Pasok and Spring Solstice Celebration Service last Sunday morning.

So, for the benefit of any parishioners who could not be there, may I just talk you through the sermon I gave about what I called "The Real Message of Easter". What I said was this: Look, no one's pretending that sometimes things don't look a bit black.

That's what we were thinking about on Good Friday. How there are times when the whole world seems full of doom and gloom, and people don't know where to turn!

But only three days later, it's a very different picture, isn't it? At least I think it is!

The sun is shining, the daffodils are out, everyone is eating Easter eggs and the little lambs are gambolling in every meadow! Well, perhaps not the lambs this year, but the underlying message remains the same!

What Easter is really telling us is that everything is under control! It's all going to turn out fine!

As it says in the Good Book, "Every cloud has a happy ending" *(Proverbs, 7.14).*

So, that's what I want to leave you with this Eastertide. The important thing is to put your trust in the Vicar, and realise that, in the end, to paraphrase the words of that great mystic St Julian of Lloyd-Webber, "All will be well that ends well."

Yours in chrisis,

Tony

PRIDE OF THE PARISH

*C*herie and I were privileged to be invited as guests-of-honour to the very moving ceremony in the parish hall to salute "Achievers of the Parish 2001", hosted by Mrs Vorderman (who presents the very popular radio show in our local hospital "Keep Smiling, You're Not Dead Yet!").

The theme of the evening was "Unsung Heroes", and I was moved to tears by the sense of humility I felt as I listened to so many tales of people's courage in adversity. And, you know, what made us feel most humble of all was to think that all these brave folk, young and old, black and white, gay and straight, were all members of the parish of which I am privileged to be the Vicar! Unfortunately, there is not room here to list all of those wonderful people (or indeed any of them!), but I assure them they remain very much in my thoughts! So, well done, all of you, whatever you did! T.B.

MILLENNIUM TENT
UPDATE

Mr Falconer writes:

Would parishioners please refrain from using the millennium tent as a skip. Today I noticed that someone has thrown an old ironing board and a microwave oven on top of it. We are still trying to find a buyer for the Tent and this does not help. So DON'T do it! *C.F.*

■ Notices

■ What a pity about the leaving party for Mrs Jay, the retiring Matron of the St Albion's Old Folks Home. Although hundreds of invitations were sent out, on the day sadly no one turned up. This was obviously a pity, since we did not have an opportunity to thank Margaret for the unique contribution she made in bossing the old people around and throwing them out of their rooms. T.B.

Dear Readers,

I wanted you all to be first to know that, as from next month (or after the PCC elections, whichever is sooner!), I shall no longer be editing this newsletter. Four years is a long time to serve in any job, and I have decided it is time for a change! So, I have decided to step down. I am sure this will come as a shock to many of you, particularly the Vicar, who may find it difficult to come up with a replacement. But, let me reassure Tony and everyone else that I will not be going far!

Although my job description may have changed, I will still be sitting in the same office and doing the same basic job, ie telling the Vicar what to do! So, it's goodbye from me, and it's hullo from me! A.C.

Tip Of The Week

Many thanks to PCC member Mr Gus Macdonald, who has sent in some very useful advice for would-be travellers: "A lot of people these days are finding it very expensive to travel by train. But there is one simple way to beat constantly rising rail fares. Go by plane instead, as I always do!"

Thank you, Gus, for such a handy tip. A £5 TV licence voucher is winging its way to you! A.C.

Parish Talking Point

A lot of parishioners are asking me these days, "Vicar, why do we still have to go on having prayers for the Royal Family? It is the year 2001, you know!"

Well, I'd like to make it clear that I personally am 100 percent behind the Queen (whatever we may think about what some of the others get up to!). But in a modern parish like ours, it is very important to keep in close touch with what ordinary people are thinking! So that is why I have asked Mr Smith (and, of course, his partner!) to organise a special "Internet Poll" to find out exactly what all of you think about this very important matter. The questions he is asking are:

A: Does it really make sense in the year 2001 to go on praying for the members of an outmoded institution based on the hereditary principle?

Or

B: Shouldn't we be praying instead for people who are more relevant to modern Britain, eg unemployed alcoholics (such as Cherie's father, Mr Booze). T.B.

ST ALBION PARISH NEWS

4th May 2001

Hullo!

Well, at least one thing we can all be grateful for – that the terrible crisis in our nation's countryside is at last completely dead and buried (unlike the cows that are piled up in the field next to the vicarage!).

So, well done everybody who helped the parish to come through what's been a very difficult time for us all, and who responded so well to my prayers that it might all somehow turn out for the best! As indeed it has, which means we can now go ahead with our PCC elections on June 7, exactly as I planned all along!

As it says in the Book of Maff, "Every cloud of smoke has a silver lining"!

But now that's all behind us, I've had time to go out and about nearer home, visiting those parts of the parish that really need a helping hand.

I am thinking in particular of the so-called "sink" estates, such as Herbert Morrison House and Chuter Ede Tower behind Pricerite.

Goodness me, it made me angry to see those beautiful blocks of flats ruined by the activities of mindless yobs.

And let's just look at that word, shall we, letter by letter? 'Y' is for 'young'. 'O' is for 'obnoxious'. 'B' is for 'badly behaved'. And 'S' is for 'sinners', a word we don't hear often enough these days.

And there's one more thing which is also highly relevant. The word 'yobs', as Cherie pointed out, is an anagram of the word 'boys'.

Which is particularly appropriate, since, let's face it, these troublemakers are nearly all male.

I can hear our friend from Tesco putting on his usual sneer and saying, "That's all very well, vicar, but what are you proposing should be done about this problem?"

Well, my answer is simple, in two words: "Crack down". 'Crack' from Greek 'krakos', meaning to do nothing. And 'down', from the Latin 'donum', meaning 'a free gift'.

Because, you know, that is surely the civilised and rational solution to the frustrations of our young people, as they roam the streets, spraying walls with their ugly daubs and throwing their beer cans into people's hedges.

Surely to goodness, it's not beyond us to bring these young

people back to a more constructive lifestyle by offering some little rewards for giving up their anti-social behaviour and doing some voluntary work around the parish, such as helping to clear away all the beer cans out of people's hedges and painting over the graffiti. I suggest that we should offer these young people a CD token or a pair of trainers.

The thought of possessing one of these coveted items would surely be enough to persuade even the most hardened young vandal or drug addict into becoming a responsible citizen? Particularly when you consider some of the titles which I hope Mr Branson might make available from the bargain bin of his record shop in the high street:

● *Wayne Sleep Sings Lloyd Webber*
● *Acker Bilk Plays The Movies*
● *Buck's Fizz Greatest Hits*

OK, youngsters, we've done our bit, it's over to you.

And maybe one day in the not too distant future, I'll be able to spell out a different version of the word 'yobs' – 'young, obedient, beautifully behaved, saved'!

Let's think about that, shall we, when we sing the new chorus I have written for this Sunday's Family Youth Service:

> *Tony's got a vision,*
> > *Tony's got a plan.*
> *Let's clean up our city*
> > *And make it spick and span.*
> *We're serving the community,*
> > *We're serving the community,*
> *We're serving the community,*
> > *That's what we're doing!*

Words and music by T. Blair (with help from Mr Campbell!)

Tony

Notices

■ Mr Robin Cook is organising a special evening at the Star of Hinduja Restaurant in the High Street to celebrate the cultural diversity of St Albion's.

There will be a wide choice of menu, viz Chicken Tikka Masala or Chicken Masala Tikka. £12.99 a head, so please book early!

A Present From The Vicar

GREAT NEWS! Every baby in the parish will be given a lump sum of £500 by the Vicar. This is a truly innovative step for St Albion's and will eradicate child poverty overnight. We take £500 from you in the new compulsory collection on Sunday. We then give it to your baby by putting it in a longterm investment account in the name of G. Brown. By the time your baby is of age, we estimate this sum will be worth at least £300 in real terms, having been invested in such blue chip companies as Railtrack, Marks & Spencer and BT. It's a great idea of mine and thanks to Gordon for coming up with it. T.B.

PARISH LAUGHS

SAY 'MONEY'

BABY BONDS

 # MY TRIP TO AMERICA

by Mr Prescott of the Working Men's Club

Contrary to various rumours, I had a most productional visit to the United States. It is true that I did not meet the Rev. Bush, the leader of the Moron Church, but I had every opportunity to explain to our American friends how strongly we here in Britain feel about the terrible problem of pollution caused by people swanning around in gas-guzzling cars, eg, Jaguars which, I would remind you all, is an American company. I also spoke to a lot of high level people (some of them on the 42nd floor of some very tall buildings) and they all listened to me very politely. J.P.

 ## Millennium Tent Latest

Charlie Falconer writes:

It is very unfortunate that the parish is now having to pay £1 million a week out of our raffle fund to a security firm to guard what remains of the Millennium Tent, and to stop people treating it as a rubbish tip.

Also, the recent heavy rain has added to our problems by causing the tent to develop severe mildew. Furthermore, the RSPCA have told us that we could face prosecution if we evict the family of foxes which have taken up residence in the IT Zone. Altogether, we would be very grateful if some benefactor could now come forward to suggest a way of keeping this magnificent structure for future generations to enjoy. C.F.

A SPECIAL MESSAGE
From Our Treasurer, Mr Brown

I have heard that there has been idle and malicious tittle-tattle round the parish to the effect that our church finances this year might turn out to be not quite so sound as I have said they would be. Let me make it absolutely clear that there is not a word of truth in these rumours. Thanks to my prudent stewardship, our bank balance is showing a satisfactory surplus of £57 billion. I have personally counted these funds twice, and I can assure you that every penny of your money is accounted for and in safe hands. I cannot, of course, guarantee that this situation will be maintained indefinitely, as unfortunately I have to rely on the competence of certain of my colleagues, such as Mr Prescott, the Vicar and the other Mr Brown. G.B.

Ladies!

With the PCC elections now only weeks away, we desperately need more ladies to come forward to lend a more 'caring' presence to our deliberations. It is quite indefensible that in the year 2001, only 35% of the places on the Council are filled by the fairer sex (if Mrs Jay will forgive the phrase!) I hope that some of our menfolk will have the decency to step down to make way for them (especially Mr Vaz!). T.B.

Prayer Of Thanks

We offer up a special prayer of gratitude this week for the courage of Cherie's sister Lauren in resisting the wiles of Satan in the form of Mr Hugh Hefner, who offered her all the riches of this world if she would only embarrass the vicar by taking her clothes off. Wise move, Lauren.

ST ALBION PARISH NEWS

17th May 2001

Hullo!

Well, there's only one thing any of us have on our minds at the moment! And that's your vicar's new spectacles!

Wherever I go in the parish, they say to me, "Goodness, Vicar, they make you look so much wiser!"

But, you know, spectacles aren't just for looking wise! They're for seeing clearly! And that's what it's all about!

Vision. Focus. Vision. And the greatest of these three is Vision.

As it says in the great *Letter of St Paul to the Electors of Corinth*, "I used to see through my glasses darkly. But now I see everything really clearly."

And that's my text as we go into this testing time of our PCC elections.

Of course, I have every confidence that you will all show your support for the present team running the parish.

I honestly don't think any group of men (and women!) could have done a better job than the team I picked four years ago (with, of course, one or two exceptions! Mr Davies, Mr Mandelson, Mr Michael, Mr Robinson, Mr Mandelson again, Mrs Mowlam and a few others may know who I'm thinking of!).

So it was in a spirit of real humility that last week I decided to take over our St Albion's Girls School for the day to brief the children and selected members of the local media on what a great job we at St Albion's have been doing!

The reason why Mr Campbell and I had chosen our local school as the best place to put over our message was not an accident.

After all, these children "are the most important people in the parish" (apart from our local journalists, of course!).

As I told them (with the flashbulbs of the St Albion Observer going off in my face!), "You are the future – and so am I!"

And that was a message they really appreciated! As one young girl said to me, "We're so glad you came today, Vicar, because if you hadn't we'd have had to be doing double maths."

I was very moved by this, and by the girls' reaction to my whole speech. The way they sat there with their eyes closed, while I told them about public-private partnerships and our longterm investment programme, showed how hard they were all concentrating!

And at the end they were all completely silent (until Mr Campbell reminded them that they should show their appreciation by clapping!).

We all then stood up and sang a new chorus which Mr Campbell had chosen for the occasion from the BBC's new song book *Hymns Modern and Modern*, and I accompanied it on my Stratocaster just to make the kids feel it was relevant to them in a very real way!

I also took my jacket off, which might have been a bit much for the headmistress, but just because I'm a vicar, it doesn't mean to say I'm not cool, and the kids went wild!

Anyway, here are the words of that hymn and I hope we will be hearing a lot more of it in the weeks to come:

> *"We are the voters of the future,*
> *We are the children of today,*
> *We are the leaders of tomorrow,*
> *We're travelling the third way."* (Repeat)

Yours (with a big X!)

Tony

The Work Goes On –
TONY'S FIVE PLEDGES

JUNE 7 is going to be a very big day for us all, when we renew those all-important vows we made four years ago.

That's why I want to add five more solemn commitments to the five we made then, making what you might call "Tony's 10 Commitments"! So here are our new pledges:

We hereby promise:

1. that we will not promise to do anything that we cannot be sure of delivering.

2. that we will not deliver anything that we haven't promised and vice versa.

3. that if there is anything we have promised that has not yet been fully delivered, we shall promise it again in the hope that nobody notices.

Unfortunately, Mr Campbell tells me that there is not enough room on this page for me to include my remaining pledges, but I PROMISE that I will try to find space for them in our next edition, provided that more important items do not have to take precedence. T.B.

✝ To Remember In Your Prayers

■ Mr Vaz, who is still unfortunately suffering from his mystery illness. We all pray that he is able to spend his time over the next few weeks in complete peace and seclusion and that when he is fully recovered he will soon find a new job. T.B.

Millennium Tent Update

Just because everyone's attention is now naturally taken up with other matters (Mr Falconer writes) that doesn't mean that we should forget our urgent need to dispose of what is left of the Millennium Tent. The foxes who were formerly living in the IT Zone have been replaced by a family of Kosovar asylum-seekers who have turned it into a Doner Kebab stall. Obviously this has added to the difficulty of selling the Tent, but prospective purchasers are reminded that this is still a wonderful bargain at 10p.

Scenes from Parish History

Thanks to Mr Bagnall for finding this old print which encapsulates everything that used to be wrong with the parish in the bad old days last century!! We wouldn't want to go back to those days would we?!! T.B.

ST ALBION PARISH NEWS

1st June 2001

Hullo!

And all I can say, as our PCC elections draw even nearer, is that the last three weeks have been the most exciting, heart-warming and truly pivotal experience I can remember since I first took charge of the parish in 1997!

Everywhere I have been in the past few weeks I have been greeted by groups of happy, smiling people, (organised by Mr Campbell) thanking me for all the good work I have put in on their behalf to make their lives better, richer and more modern in every way.

Who says that no one cares any more and that no one is interested in turning out to meet the vicar? Who says no-one wants to hear the "good news" – the news of a new world in which everyone works together to build a fairer society for all? A world not just for the better off but the rich as well?

Time and again I was impressed by the sheer number of people who turned out to see me. For example, in our local hospital, they had been literally queuing up for months, and "so great was the multitude", as it says in the Bible, that they were spilling out onto trolleys in the corridors and wheelchairs in the car park!

As I said to them, "Blessed are those who wait, for they shall see God rather sooner than they expected!" *(Book of the Dead, Ch. VI, 12).*

It's a pity that one woman had to spoil the afternoon for everybody by insisting on coming up and shouting at me, just because her "partner" was dying for lack of medical attention.

And what a pity she chose to make such an unfortunate fuss in front of our friends from the media, who Mr Campbell had spent weeks organising to film my visit and to show how much the church listens to ordinary people.

Eventually I managed to calm her down by telling her than I was only there to help, and that by the year 2015 the parish would be allocating an additional 15 percent a year to the hospital fund, which would achieve precisely the improved care she was asking for.

As I told her, it's all a matter of resources, which comes of course from the original Greek, "reskos", meaning "sorry", and "orkis", meaning "no money".

Sadly, the lady in question wasn't prepared to listen and stormed off before she could hear my words of comfort (which of course comes from the original Aramaic "Com" or "go", and "fort", "on thy way"). Frankly, that good lady reminded me all too vividly of another, rather older woman in our parish who would be equally well advised to hold her peace these days.

I am talking, of course, of my predecessor, the Deaconess Thatcher, who is, alas, in a state of some confusion nowadays, due to her advancing age and dependence on alcohol.

She has seen fit, for some reason known only to herself, to allege that I somehow still cling on to the old discredited beliefs. Things like helping the poor, tending the sick and fighting against injustice! Honestly, no-one believes in any of that stuff any more, least off all me!

All I can say is that I have shown considerable patience with this particular previous incumbent, and that it really is time for us all to move on, particularly her – perhaps to another life!

And talking of moving on, I have composed a new chorus for our service of thanksgiving for the victory in the PCC elections (I hope that isn't presumptious of me!!).

Moving on, moving on,
From the place where we have gone.
Don't look back, just look ahead,
These are the words the vicar said.
Chorus
Move on, move on,
Move on, move on,
Sharron, Darren and Yvonne
(or the congregation may sing other names, eg, Matthew, Mark, Luke and John)

So this is the message I have been trying to put over to the parish in recent weeks. I am not for a minute saying that we have done everything that we promised we were going to do! No. That is why we need another five years so that we can keep those promises over the years that lie ahead!

Look! We are not complacent. Far from it! Just because we are going to get the overwhelming support of everyone in the parish, that does not mean we should be complacent in any way!

Indeed, we should be humble when we contemplate the pride we rightly take in all that we have achieved!

That is why I urge you all to make "the sign of the cross" alongside the names of all my team on the Big Day!

Yours ever, Tony

CUT OUT AND DISPLAY THIS POSTER IN YOUR WINDOW! NOW! A.C.

PCC ELECTIONS

More T? Yes, more T-ony is the only way forward for the Parish! Be sensible – support the man with the honest mug!

MR PRESCOTT – A STATEMENT

■ A lot of people have written to me complaining about the recent incident involving our good friend Mr Prescott of the Working Men's Club and a parishioner Mr Evans. Of course, I cannot condone Mr Prescott's behaviour on this occasion, but we must remember that John is John, ie a bit of a rough diamond who did not have the benefit of a decent education and is therefore prone to express himself through his fists, rather than through the kind of debating skills for which a career as the barman in a working men's club scarcely equips you! T.B.

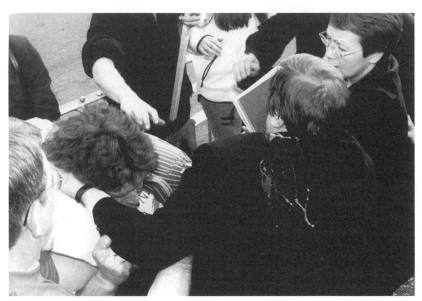

"Fight the Good Fight" (John 1.2). Mr Prescott leads with his left (a pity, as the right is always better!) and convinces Mr Evans that he is really listening to his argument in a meaningful way. T.B.

Mr Prescott's Famous Recipe

Homemade Punch

Directions
1. Take one egg
2. Then don't take any more
3. Boil over
4. Beat furiously
5. Get separated
6. Scramble words
7. Cool down slowly

 And there you have it! A nice strong Punch to help the party along. *Serves no-one.*

CHERIE — AN APOLOGY

MAY I apologise to all Tony's parishioners for the fact that I have not been "out and about" with Tony in the parish these last few weeks. This is because I have been working on a very important case in my job as a lawyer, defending one of our most respected local multi-national chemical companies against the attempts by various greedy parishioners to get more pension money out of them! Honestly! And, anyway, why should I be paraded around the parish just because I am the Vicar's wife. The Vicar doesn't need me to help, as he proves every night when he gets up to look after the baby!

Cherie Booth

PS. If anyone wants my personal help on any legal matters, contact me on my mobile: 07103 456789. Usual rates apply.

ST ALBION PARISH NEWS

15th June 2001

Sadly, there is no room this week to print the usual picture of the church. Instead we have a charming photo of the vicar telling parishioners that they should concentrate on the issues and not on personalities

Hullo!

And what a wonderful week for the parish this has been!

And of course I don't just mean for me personally, but for all those unsung heroes (and heroines!) behind the scenes who have done all the small but essential jobs which you don't hear about – keeping the tea urn warm, arranging the flowers, hoovering up the biscuits in the creche and looking after the parish finances.

I am sure our treasurer Mr Brown will not mind if I don't single him out for special praise, because there are so many others who have done so much in so many ways, with a lot less thanks than Mr Brown has had!

Above all, this has been a team effort, from the Greek "teamos", meaning a "wise leader" and "effortikos", meaning "who does it all by himself".

I met one parishioner over the weekend who couldn't wait to

shake my hand, and said "Vicar, you must be very, very proud – this is a real personal triumph for you!"

Well, I hear what she says (and I agree with it!). But at the same time I think it is very important that one doesn't get big-headed about being the most popular and successful vicar the parish has ever had!

That's why I am rather dubious about the suggestion made by so many of you that my name should go forward for beatification.

It is kind of them to point out that I have already performed the necessary two miracles, at two successive PCC elections!

But, really, I think we all should wait a bit, before rushing into the sanctification business!

I know "St Anthony" has rather a ring to it! But let's just keep it to "Rev. Tony" for the time being, shall we?

Tony

Women's Group

Mrs Jowell writes:

Thanks to the Vicar's initiative, there are going to be more women than ever on the PCC – Ms Morris, Ms Hewitt, Ms Beckett and myself, to name but all of us!

My own responsibility will be to look at ways to organise people's leisure time – they seem to have far too much of it and appear to spend it by eating, drinking and enjoying themselves in an unstructured way. From now on, I will be trying to turn people's "Free Time" into something more productive. T.J.

Valete

It's a sad day for us all as we say farewell to Mr Chris Smith who has been in charge of the St Albion's Arts Festival and the new unbuilt Under 11 football pitch on the wasteland behind the cemetery. Many of you have expressed your regret at his leaving and seem to think he has done a marvellous job. This may well be so, but I happen to know that Mr Smith wanted to spend more time with his family even though he hasn't got one. T.B.

A Warning from Mr Blunkett, new Head of Neighbourhood Watch

Whatever you are doing, stop it!
Because I am watching you.
Signed Lucy the Dog,
pp. Mr Blunkett

Service Of Humble Thanksgiving For A Great Victory

PEAL OF BELLS
(starting six in the morning and continuing all day)
Ringers: A. Darling, S. Byers, A. Milburn

ANTHEM
See The Conquering Hero Comes
(attrib. T. Blair)

Procession from the coffee area to the altar

BIDDING PRAYER
(the Vicar)
"Brothers and sisters, we give thanks for this, our crushing landslide, and in a spirit of deep humility we rejoice in the destruction of all our enemies, as they are cast down into the pit, and from thenceforth into outer darkness for ever and ever. Amen."

RESPONSES
ALL: Alleluia, allelulia!
VICAR: We are re-elected!
ALL: We are re-elected indeed!

CREED
ALL: We do not believe in very much, but we do believe in the re-election. Amen.
VICAR: Thanks be to the Lord Levy.
ALL: And all our other sponsors!

HYMN
(Chorus)
We have overcome, we have overcome,
We have overcome this day.
Deep in our hearts we do believe
It's thanks to the third way!

THE BLESSING
VICAR: Bless you all!
ALL: No – bless *you*, Vicar!
VICAR: Would you all now stand for the Recession.

Order of Service printed free of charge by R. Desmond, publishers of adult multi-ethnic literature, by appointment to the Vicar.

Parish Letters

Dear Sir,

May I be allowed to put the record straight regarding my promotion. It is quite untrue that I had angry words with the Vicar over his decision to give my post as organist to Mr Straw, even though, as everyone knows, he is completely useless and not nearly as clever as me. My new job handing out the hymn sheets is actually a much more important job than Mr Straw's, involving a detailed

> *Yours faithfully (providing I keep the house),*
> *Robin Cook*

The Editor reserves the right to cut all correspondence from people who are not important any more. A.C.

❖ Important People in the Parish ❖

An occasional series by local artist Mr de la Nougerede.

No.1 Mr Straw

ST ALBION PARISH NEWS

29th June 2001

Brothers and Sisters!

A very warm welcome to this newsletter, particularly to all those new readers who may be coming to it for the first time after all the huge interest generated by the recent PCC elections!

The first point that I want to make loud and clear is that I am listening!

This is a listening parish with a listening vicar!

That is why I was so upset when our recent oecumenical meeting in Gothenburg (a lovely city by the way!) was ruined by the antics of a tiny minority of 20,000 hooligans intent on making trouble.

There was no excuse at all for this display of childish anarchy, and it was totally untrue to suggest, as some people did, that we churchmen have lost touch with ordinary people and spend all our time swanning around from one conference to another.

This is an outrageous lie, and I do not want to hear it again from anyone!

As for being out of touch, I can be contacted at any time of day or night on my website, www.albion.co.uk.eu

Or you can contact my secretary Mrs Hunter ('Anji') by writing to her at the vicarage, and she will make sure that you receive a printed acknowledgement in no more than six weeks!

And what nonsense these silly demonstrators were shouting. I saw one banner which read "You cannot serve God and Mammon". How offensive that was to the hard-working members of our business community, and how right the Swedish police were to shoot them in the back!

But enough of these tiresome distractions from the real business of how I am getting on with running the parish over the next five years.

Obviously, there is not enough space here to describe my plans in detail. But here are some of the main points:

1. The PCC has unanimously agreed to increase my stipend by £60,000 a year in recognition of my heavy workload (and may I remind some of you that I said "no" to a pay increase over the past four years, when a lot of people [ie, teachers, nurses, etc] had whopping 1.5 percent performance-related pay increases!).

2. To look really closely at a lot of things which need attention and

to make sure that we get these things right as soon as possible, with the aid of our local business community who have so much to contribute (and not just to our parish funds!).

3. Look, I said there wasn't enough space to go into detail. But it's all on the vicarage website, so if you want to know all the rest, just "log on" now! ("Log on" being the old Greek word for "website".)

As we sing in the chorus at evensong, to the tune of that wonderful old football hymn:

> *Log on, log on, with hope in your heart,*
> *And you'll never be alone.*
> *You'll always be with Tone!*

100 INTERNET HYMNS FOR TODAY

Your cyberfriend!

Tony

The new PCC gets down to business – and look how many women there are!! Especially near the camera! Well done to all you ladies! T.B.

Forthcoming Talks With Slides

A number of PCC members have kindly agreed to give talks on their new areas of responsibility.

- **Mrs Beckett will talk about the countryside under the title "Through A Caravan Window".**

- **Mr Byers will talk about "My First Car, Which I Will Buy As Soon As I Learn To Drive".**

- **Mr Caborn will be answering your questions on sport – easy ones only please (!) i.e. no football or rugby or cricket ot tennis or athletics or any other sport.**

Millennium Tent Update

Following the recent PCC elections, it has been decided that we should draw a line under the problems of the Millennium Tent. In future, there will be no mention of the Tent in these pages ever again, particularly not the fact that it is still unsold, is costing £1 million a week to parish funds and has recently been made the subject of a "Dangerous Structure Notice". C.F.

Mr Prescott Writes From The Working Men's Club

It is completely untrue to say that I have been demoted in some way in the recent reshuffle of PCC responsibilities. On the contrary, the Vicar has personally asked me to write a 1000-word piece for this newsletter on my vital new role organising all the administrative affairs of

The Editor reserves the right to cut all pieces on the grounds of space, particularly those from people who have been demoted. A.C.

✠ To Remember In Your Prayers

Mrs Hoey, who did such a good job of messing up our parish sports day and is now going round claiming that she was unfairly sacked from her job on the PCC. Let us pray that Mrs Hoey loses the power of speech for a while, to teach her a lesson in humility that she will not forget! T.B.

ST ALBION PARISH NEWS

13th July 2001

Hullo!

What a wonderful spell of hot weather we've been enjoying since the PCC elections! Coincidence? Well...!

And, naturally, after all the hard work we've been putting in over the last few months, our thoughts are turning to the all-important question of where we're going to spend our holidays.

"I expect you'll be off with your fancy friends in Italy as per usual, Vicar?" said our friend in Tesco, standing next to their new GM-free Organic Dips and Nibbles display.

"Well, no, that's just where you're wrong, chum," I was able to inform him.

"On the contrary, Cherie and I have decided to set an example and to do our bit for the hard-pressed tourist industry of our own country.

"That is why, for the record, we are going to spend a whole night in Mrs Woodward's B&B establishment, right at the heart of beautiful Humbugside."

It may not sound much, but my goodness, if everyone in the parish was to follow our lead, what a boost it would give to all the good folk who, through no fault of their own, have to live in the English countryside, surrounded by greedy farmers and dead sheep!

Of course, after this we'll need a proper holiday, so it'll be "buon giorno" to our dear friends, the Count Fribi and his delightful wife Fribiza, who have once again agreed to put us up at their modest little 840-bedroom *palazzo* on the shores of Lake Berlusconi.

I don't mind telling you, Cherie and I are particularly looking forward to getting away from some of the older parishioners, like Mr Skinner, who behaved appallingly at last week's evensong when I was trying to say a few words about our new policy on providing charitable help for the disabled.

All I said was that it seemed perfectly reasonable to check up on someone you've given money to, to make sure that, if they claim to be disabled, then they really are.

If someone says they are visually impaired, for instance, like Mr Blunkett, then it is only right and proper to give him a sight test every three years, to make sure that he is genuinely blind and not just trying to get a free dog!

But no sooner had I begun to explain this than Mr Skinner and his friends started shouting "What about you and your rich friends, Vicar? Shouldn't you check up on them first, before you persecute the poor?"

Honestly! It's not as if I have the time to get to church very often these days. So when I do turn up, the least people could do is to show a bit of reverence and listen to what I have to say without interruption!

Look! I really do despair of some of these older members of the parish who obviously haven't begun to understand everything we've been trying to do since I took over the parish four years ago!

Can I just remind them of a few texts which they can study while they are waiting in some airport lounge for their package flight to Johnmajorca or wherever they are going:

"Blessed are the rich, for they shall inherit" *(The Platitudes)*

"It is easier for a rich man to enter a hospital than a poor man" *(Book of Bupa, 14.6)*

"The first shall be first, and the last shall be on a waiting list" *(Gospel according to St Margaret, 7.5)*

"It is perfectly possible to serve two masters, the public and the private sector" *(Letter to the Shareholders, 3.1)*

Have a nice (holi)day!

Your friend,

✝ To Remember In Your Prayers

Mr Hattersley, one of our old-age pensioners, who is unfortunately suffering from senile dementia brought on by over-eating. It is not his fault that he lives in the past, and cannot appreciate all the good things that are happening now! Give him the courage to know that he is totally wrong about everything, and the strength to keep his mouth shut (except when he's putting food in it!). T.B.

Scenes from Parish Life

Thanks to Mr De la Nougerede for his charming drawing of the game of musical chairs we had at the vicarage party to celebrate winning the PCC elections! T.B.

Parish Film Soc.

Mr Howells, the new projectionist, writes:

I've had enough of all these stuffy, snobby, toffee-nosed British heritage films! From now on I will be showing only modern, realistic, relevant films like "Trainspotting". Here is the Summer schedule:

July: Trainspotting
Aug: Trainspotting
Sep: Trainspotting

The Autumn season is cancelled.

Kim Howells

Lines From A Local Poet

I'm a fighter,
not a quitter,
I'm not angry,
I'm not bitter,
So now I'm
waiting by the
phone,
Please can I have my job back, Tone?

P. Mandelson,
The Old Cottage,
Hartlepool Road.

Mrs Mowlam's Summer Recipe
Cannabis Summer Pudding

Ingredients:
2lbs assorted soft summer fruit
1lb organic sliced bread
2oz finest Afghan Black
6oz sugar

Instructions
Throw away fruit, bread, sugar. Light up remainder, and enjoy!

WARNING: This recipe is illegal at present, but I am open to argument about its consumption in limited private circumstances. D. Blunkett, Chairman, Neighbourhood Watch.

My Day Out
by Mr Caborn

I had a very boring day at a place called Wimbledon, where they play this game called tennis. What happens is that one person hits a ball and then another person hits it back. It goes on for a long time, and then you have strawberries in a tent. For me this was the best bit, because I hate sport!

R. Caborn (aged 52)

ST ALBION PARISH NEWS

27th July 2001

Hullo!

As you all know, I have recently been setting out some very important new proposals for the reorganisation of the parish and the way we run our services.

At the heart of my restructuring of St Albion's is the idea that our local businesses can join forces with us, to create the kind of vibrant, pivotal church for the 21st century that we all want.

The sort of ideas we've been discussing are really exciting. For instance:

● THE SPONSORED PEW SCHEME, under which local businessmen such as Mr Murdoch of the Adult Vids and Mags Centre donate money for the upkeep of the pews, in return for which each seat will have a hassock embroidered with the logo of the firm concerned.

● PARISH COFFEE MORNINGS. These will in future be franchised to our high street coffee shop The Cappuccino Experience. This makes good house-keeping sense.

● SUNDAY SCHOOL. As parents know, we have had only limited space in the vestry for our very popular kids inter-faith workshop sessions. But the manager of McDonald's fast food has volunteered to put his premises at our disposal. This will enable our toddlers to learn about not only the familiar bible stories, but also the very important world of "shakes 'n' fries"!

● MAKING BETTER USE OF THE CHURCH TOWER. As you know, we have already arranged an auction for mobile phone companies to bid for use of our church tower as a telecommunications mast (please – no more letters on the possible health hazards, as these have been fully investigated by Mr Campbell, and only a tiny percentage of children get leukaemia). But it has now been proposed that we should offer the tower to Mr Bush for use as a rocket-launching pad as part of his Star Wars plan.

Hey, these are just a few of the exciting ideas that we are now kicking around at PCC meetings.

But, unfortunately, there are still a few diehards among our older parishioners, like Mr Morris and Mr Edmunds, who see all these new proposals as in some way a threat to the cosy way of life they have been used to for far too long.

Look, it's time these people realised that there's no such thing as a job for life any longer! Even I don't expect to be your vicar for more than perhaps another 20 years!

So, what I say to the Morrises and Edmundses of our parish is what I say to all the cynics and the doubters who are blind to all our amazing achievements since I became your vicar four years ago: as Our Lord himself said, "Get a life"!

This is such an important message that I have based a chorus on it, to be sung at the evening service this Sunday once our "Body and Soul" Aerobics Class (sponsored by Holland and Barrett) has dispersed.

CHORUS
> *For everyone who's living,*
> *Be they husband, be they wife,*
> *Get a life! Get a life!*
>
> *No matter how you're feeling,*
> *Whether happy or in strife,*
> *Get a life! Get a life!*
>
> *When you're sitting at your table*
> *With your fork and spoon and knife,*
> *Get a life! Get a life!*

(Words and music, T. Blair)

See you around! *Tony*

BLESS YOU!

The Vicar of Dibley drops in at the vicarage with a donation for Comic Relief. Says Rev French: "I've always been a great fan of Tony. He always makes me laugh when I see him on the telly."

Congratulations...

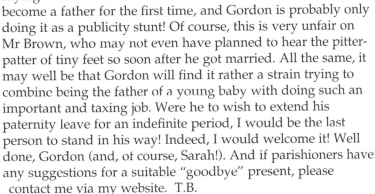

... to our treasurer Mr Brown and his new wife on the announcement that they are expecting a happy event! I know that some people are saying that 50 is far too old to become a father for the first time, and Gordon is probably only doing it as a publicity stunt! Of course, this is very unfair on Mr Brown, who may not even have planned to hear the pitter-patter of tiny feet so soon after he got married. All the same, it may well be that Gordon will find it rather a strain trying to combine being the father of a young baby with doing such an important and taxing job. Were he to wish to extend his paternity leave for an indefinite period, I would be the last person to stand in his way! Indeed, I would welcome it! Well done, Gordon (and, of course, Sarah!). And if parishioners have any suggestions for a suitable "goodbye" present, please contact me via my website. T.B.

 ## Parish Postbag

Dear Sir,

I would like to protest in the strongest possible terms at the disgraceful treatment of my American friend Mr Kiley. He has very kindly come over here to help us out in any way he can and the Vicar and Mr Brown have behaved shabbily and with a total lack of

> *Yours sincerely,*
> *KEN LIVINGSTONE,*
> *Newts R Us Aquatic Pet*
> *Centre (and Chair High*
> *Street Traffic Action Group)*

The Editor reserves the right to cut letters for reasons of lack of space. A.C.

COMMITTEE ROUND-UP

The vicar writes: I am pleased to make it clear that it was never my intention that Mrs Dunwoody and Mr Anderson should be removed from their posts as chairpersons of two of our important committees. This was entirely due to a misunderstanding of some remarks I made about "getting rid of the troublemakers" which of course I did not make. Many parishioners wrote in to protest and to call for the reinstatement of the people who I never meant to remove, so they have now been reinstated on the committees in question, albeit in a different capacity, and I do not wish to hear any more nonsense about this. R.C.

ST ALBION PARISH NEWS

10th August 2001

Hullo!

Or should I say buon giorno, buenos días and hasta la vista?

As you will know from the notes handed out with last week's service sheets, Cherie and I are spending a few weeks going round the world, spreading the good news and making new friends for St Albion's wherever we go!

It's not for me to say, but everyone tells me that we have been a terrific success all over South America!

They're calling me "the first global vicar" and Cherie "the new Queen of Hearts". She's far too modest, of course, to accept any silly comparisons with Princess Diana (you may remember I read the lesson rather movingly at her funeral!).

But I can tell you that when it comes to picking up homeless slum toddlers and giving them a big hug in front of the cameras, she leaves the late Princess standing!

And let me say straightaway to our friend from Tesco, whom I can already hear sneering in his usual unhelpful way as he emerges from behind the GM-free Kiwi Fruit 'n' Nut Cereal counter, that Cherie and I are not, repeat *not* on holiday!

No, this is very definitely parish business, and we will be spending our real holiday at home, ie the home of our very good friends the Prince and Princess Fribini in Tuscany.

And, of course, I'm not forgetting my promise that we shall also be spending some of our holiday in the English countryside, as a gesture of solidarity with all those poor farmers who are going round infecting their sheep in the hope of getting generous compensation!

And I have every intention of keeping that promise! If we can find a spare day or two in my diary, when we come back from our various oecumenical trips overseas, and so long as parish business allows, I assure you all that I have every intention of nipping down to the west country for a short time to have my picture taken for this newsletter!

But, hey, enough of holidays and back to business!

Cherie and I had a fantastic day looking at some amazing waterfalls in Brazil and Argentina (if any parishioners ever find themselves over there, I can tell you, it certainly makes bed and breakfast in Torquay look pretty dull!).

We enjoyed meeting our opposite numbers in Argentina, Monsignor Cardozo and Cardinal de la Rua, who gave us a tremendous welcome!

We discussed all sorts of subjects over various meals, which included lots of delicious local steaks! And, incidentally, what a pleasure it was to be in a country which very sensibly vaccinates all its animals against foot-and-mouth and then exports them to England! Our farmers have certainly got a lot to learn from our Argentinian amigos!

I would like to write more about all our adventures, but unfortunately Cherie and I have to go off to an urgent tango demonstration!

I tell you, these oecumenical trips are no picnic (although we are going on one tomorrow in the famous Andes mountains!).

You can rest assured that the parish has been in good hands while I've been away, because I did not think it was necessary to ask Mr Prescott to stand in for me on this occasion.

In the age of globalisation and the mobile telephone, I can continue to keep an eye on what's going on in St Albion's, even when I am on holiday (which I am not!).

As we say in these parts, "Vaya con Dios" (which is the Argentinian for "enjoy"!). *Antonio*

<u>HAPPY CLAPPY</u>

The vicar's wife meets a group of children in Mexico and teaches them some English hymns. "He's got the Whole Globalised World in his hands, he's got the Whole etc. etc." A.C.

A Message From Mrs Beckett, Chair of the Parish Farmers Liaison Committee

I will not be available to listen to any more complaints about the so-called "crisis in the country-side" as I am spending the next five weeks touring the French countryside in my caravan. Frankly, it will be a great relief to be in a country where they do not have foot-and-mouth, and I am looking forward to our first plate of cotelettes d'agneau et frites!

Mrs Beckett
Somewhere in the
Dordogne.

IMPORTANT NOTICE

From Mrs Beverley Hughes, chair of the St Albion's Viewers and Listeners Action Group

Have you heard about a TV programme that is so outrageous and disgusting that it should be banned? Please let me know, and I will do everything I can to get it taken off the air at once. I do emphasise that you don't have to have watched this programme yourself (and I certainly won't!). B.H.

✝ To Remember In Your Prayers

...the Italian police who did such a good job in protecting our recent oecumenical gathering in Genoa. They have been subjected to a lot of hurtful criticism for the highly disciplined way in which they dealt with a lot of irresponsible troublemakers while they lay asleep, dreaming of the overthrow of western civilisation. It is outrageous for these anarchists and other criminal elements to pretend that they had been beaten up or even in one case killed by the conscientious carabinieri who were only doing their job. T.B.

Parish Postbag

Dear Vicar,
You are a scrounger and a toadying lickspittle of the imperialist warmonger Bush. The only thing you enjoy is killing people. You are far worse than Milosevic and
Yours,
H. Pinter,
C/o The Caretaker,
Antonia Fraser House,
Sidcup Road.

The editor reserves the right to cut all the letters for reasons of space. A.C.

ST ALBION PARISH NEWS

24th August 2001

WISH WE WEREN'T HERE

Greetings from the West Country! (Or should that be the "wet country"?) It's raining all the time, the food's ghastly and there's nothing to do! But fortunately we're only here to have our picture taken before we fly off to France!

Everyone we met in Cornwall said "Hey, Vicar, where did you get that fantastic tan? Obviously not round here!" Of course, I didn't let on that it was thanks to our "working trip" to sunny Mexico! Fortunately, I gather nothing too serious has happened in the parish while we've been away, although if it had, I am always on call, 24 hours a day, via e-mail on my laptop! Euan says "Cheers" to all his mates!

Yours,

Tony

(and Cherie of course!)

Salve!
(or "Welcome", as we say nowadays!)

This month we welcome Mr Birt, who has kindly agreed to come in, on a voluntary basis, to advise us how to run the parish more efficiently, and to give the team ministry a "forward planning capability". John has already come up with some really brilliant ideas.

For instance, the PCC is to be broken down into a series of individual working modules, each with its own specific remit and interacting with the others through a central co-ordination unit. To give an illustration of how this will help to streamline parish administration, I have asked John to sketch out how this will work with the flower roster.

Mr Birt writes: *The flower roster will be divided into three roster directorates. The first will originate the "floral resource" (the flowers) and sell them on an internal market basis to the second directorate which will be responsible for "the vase resource" (vases, stands, etc) which they will lease out in turn to the third or "display directorate", in charge of creative arrangements for the presentation of the floral resource to the consumers (ie, the congregation). The quality of the display will be monitored by a fourth directorate, which I have only just thought of, which will take account of such criteria as cost budgeting, consumer response, sustainability and overall human resource efficiency. This is intended to serve as a working template for other areas of parish reorganisation, eg the After Service Coffee To Biscuits supply chain, the Hymn Sheet Resource Distribution Network, the Ongoing Hassock Repair and Replacement Programme and the Strimming and General Maintenance of the Deceased Waste Disposal and Landfill Zone (formerly "the graveyard"). J.B.*

A great start, John! And surely this should silence all those malicious parishioners who have been putting it about that Mr Birt is nothing more than a brainless bureaucrat, who has only been given the job because he is a friend of Mr Mandelson's!

MORE CREAM TEA, VICAR?

Tony and Cherie are served up a traditional Cornish holiday treat. Mmm! Scones, strawberry jam and lashings of clotted cream! What a pity they didn't have time to eat any of it before catching their plane to France. A.C.

HARVEST FESTIVAL

I have put Mr Haskins in charge of the arrangements for this year's Harvest Festival. Over to you, Chris!

"This year I do not want to see the church full of homegrown rubbish from people's gardens. All those mis-shapen marrows, baskets of dirty fruit and pots of badly made jam with mould on the top are totally out of place in a modern church. This is not what the harvest is about nowadays. If you want to make a contribution this year, could you bring in items which really reflect modern agricultural production, eg: chicken massala TV dinners, mechanically-recovered meat pies, Express Dairies UHT low-fat milk and GM rice-style soya bean finger nibbles. All these items are available at shopper-friendly prices from my superstore on the High Street.

So, remember, for this year's Harvest Festival you can't get better value than Northern Foods (Motto: 'The taste to die for')."

Thanks, Chris! Sounds as if we're really on our way with this one! And I'd just add one more thing! We certainly don't want any whingeing farmers at this year's service, spoiling it for everyone else. As Chris himself has rightly said, the sooner all these farmers get a job on a BMW production line the better! T.B.

A lovely drawing of Mr Prescott reading the church notices in the absence of the vicar (not that he is absent – thanks to e-mail and mobile phone "He is always with you!"). Thanks to local artist Mr De la Nougerede for this happy image of John! A.C.

ST McDONALD'S PARISH NEWS
(formerly St Albion Parish News)
7th September 2001

Just for this issue we have decided to replace the usual picture of the church with something a bit more modern and forward-looking. Hence this charming picture of a cheeseburger. A.C. Editor.

A POSTCARD FROM THE VICAR...

CHATEAU DE SADE

Swish You Were Here

Bonjour!

Or rather it isn't a particularly bon jour, thanks to a very silly story which I gather is circulating round the parish that the very modest little chateau that we are staying in, belonging to a very good friend of ours who happens to be a judge, was once used as the set for a pornographic film.

Honestly, why can't people just grow up! You would think the parishioners of St Albion's might have more important things on their mind, like the fact that there won't be any teachers at the St Albion's Primary School when the new term begins, or the fact that several parishioners are having to go to Germany to get their hips replaced.

Everybody knows that I won't have anything to do with the disgusting and perverted business of pornography. I am no more involved in pornography than my good friend Mr Desmond, who runs Dirty Des's Adult Magazine Mart in the High Street and . has been such a keen supporter of everything we are trying to do in the parish.

It would be nice if, just for a change, Cherie and I and the boys could get away for a few months without nasty and small-minded parish gossips spreading rumours about me trying to wangle a cheapo holiday when we were in Cornwall.

I went out of my way to visit the West Country, a place that we would not normally think of going to, to set an example in the parish. You'd think the least the Nare Hotel would have done in the circumstances was to offer us a small discount, say 50 per cent – not unreasonable, is it?

Especially since our friend Mr Keane has given us a 100 per cent discount to stay here in France, as did our good friends the Count and Contessa di Fribi when we stayed at their house in Italy.

No wonder no one goes on holiday in England! It is so much more expensive than the Continent, not to mention the rain, the terrible food and the fact that it takes you forever to get there. No, for my money (or rather not!) there's nothing like La Belle France any day! Au revoir (unfortunately)

Votre ami

Antoine

HARVEST FESTIVAL UPDATE

Mr Haskins writes: *Thank you for your wonderful response to my plans for our new-look harvest festival!*
I have now had an even better idea.

We shall be replacing the altar for our service with a giant freezer-cabinet (supplied by courtesy of my own company Northern Foods!). This will ensure the best possible display of your harvest offerings, including any of the following "Harvest Specials": Chicken 'n' Cheese Krispy Dippers ("yes, ch-e-e-e-se!"), Pork-Style Chicken Tikka Masala ("Give us some more, Mum!"), Turkey-Flavoured Yoghurt ("Kids 'gobble" it up!").

Herring 'n' Marmite Mini-Pizzas ("I think I'm going to be sick!").

All these items are of course available to parishioners at a special discount price from my superstore on the High Street.

FURTHER THOUGHTS ON PARISH RE-ORGANISATION

A memo from Mr Birt

As part of Phase Two of my plans for rationalising the church timetable and optimising our resource management strategy, I have proposed that in the future we should amalgamate Easter and Christmas (to be known in the future as Christ-er or East-mas, according to focus group response). This is because audience figures show that these are the two "Key Events" which produce the highest ratings.

By merging them intoone "Super Event" we can look to halving the cost base (candles, trees, cribs etc.) while retaining full audience share.

Thank you, John! Keep the ideas coming! TB

Thought For The Day

How sad it always is to see friends falling out, even when they have in the past been rude about the vicar of their parish!

It is particularly sad when they resort to calling each other abusive names, such as "Fatty", "Baldy", "Hanger And Flogger" and "Euro-Lover". How even sadder it would be if people got so fed up with both of them for their childish behaviour that they decided never to have anything to do with either of them again!

Let us all hope and pray that this happens! (Is this right? A.C.)

T.B. (via email!)

HYMNS MODERN AND MODERN

(Additional Anthems and Choruses for Parish Use)

No. 94

TO BE SUNG IN TIMES OF CRISIS

Fight the good fight against the right
> *The forces of conservatism have been put to flight*
Just trust in Tony and you will see
> *Things will get better eventually.*

(Words T. Blair)

No. 95

A HYMN FOR SUSTAINABLE DEVELOPMENT

There is a greenfield site far away
> *Without a city wall*
But since everyone needs a place to live
> *We're going to build over it all.*

(Words J. Prescott)

No. 96

A HYMN FOR HARVEST FESTIVAL

We plough the fields and scatter
> *The dead sheep on the land,*
For they have all been slaughtered
> *By MAFF's almighty hand.*

(Words Mrs Beckett)

Parish Scrapbook

A look at events in St Albion's over the last year.
Compiled by Alastair Campbell

THE VICAR' S BACK!!! Tony returns from a long weekend in the country ready to take on the responsibilities of the modern vicar. "You are the rock and roll on which I shall build my church" (Book of Levi-ticus, 17.3)

Hats off to Cherie! The Vicar's wife proves that big cheques are always in fashion here at St Albion's and she puts poor Mrs Prescott in the shade – which isn't surprising under that hat. Good for you, Cherie!

A lovely picture of Cherie surrounded by this year's successful 'A' Level students from St Albion School For Girls, all of whom have 7 Grade As each! Well done to everyone but particularly the vicar for such marvellous results

The vicar attends one of the many "Blair Groups" that have sprung up in the parish over the last four years. This is a women-only meeting dedicated to collective worship over a simple plate of ciabatta and a cup of decaffeinated semi-skimmed cappuccino. The vicar is telling the ladies how important it is for women to make their voices heard and not just sit around letting men do all the talking!

More e-mail vicar? Tony is right up-to-date with all the latest technology. Here he demonstrates how to log-on to the vicarage website www.albion.co.uk.eu It's what we computer experts call a hit!

TB or not TB? That is the question! And luckily an overwhelming proportion of the parish (22%) have decided in a poll that Mr Blair was the only answer! Hurrah for our "acting" vicar!

The answer my friend is blowing in the wind

Let's close with a charming portrait of the vicar hitting all the right notes (!) by local artist Mr Redway.

As Tony says,
"I am the Beginning and the End"(!)
A.C.